ABOUT THE COMPILERS

Bill and Marta Annett together run a small consultancy in London. Bill served in the Royal Artillery during the 1939–45 war, after which he spent twenty-five years in advertising and public relations, before setting up the present partnership.

Marta is Hungarian, born and brought up in Budapest during the difficult years of the thirties and forties and provides the logic, judgment and critical ability essential to a man-and-wife operation.

Lifelong defenders of animals and of their place in society, Bill and Marta have worked for many years to promote the realistic concept of replacing live animal experimentation by alternative methods.

Also by Bill and Marta Annett
Winning Through

FOR THE LOVE
OF ANIMALS
True Stories from the Famous

Compiled by
Bill and Marta Annett

ARROW BOOKS

Grateful acknowledgement is made for permission
to quote from the following works:

The Best of Friends by John Aspinall (Macmillan)
Animals in War by Jilly Cooper (Heinemann)
The Stationary Ark by Gerald Durrell (Collins)
Down to Earth by HRH Prince Philip, Duke of Edinburgh (Collins)
The Cats of Shambala by Tippi Hedren (Century Hutchinson)
The Bells of Heaven by Ralph Hodgson (Macmillan)
Tsi Tsa by George Mikes (André Deutsch)
Next Panda Please by David Taylor (Unwin Hyman)
500 Mile Walkies by Mark Wallington (Arrow)

Extracts were also used from the following books
by kind permission of the authors:

Sensible Pets and Silly People by M. Raymonde-Hawkins
Animals and Man by The Hon. Miriam Rothschild

Arrow Books Limited
62–65 Chandos Place, London WC2N 4NW

An imprint of Century Hutchinson Limited

London Melbourne Sydney Auckland
Johannesburg and agencies throughout
the world

First published in 1989

Printed and bound in Great Britain by
The Guernsey Press Co Ltd
Guernsey, C.I.

Phototypeset by Input Typesetting Ltd, London SW19 8DR

ISBN 0 09 965060 6

THE BELLS OF HEAVEN

'Twould ring the bells of Heaven
The wildest peal for years
If Parson lost his senses
And people came to theirs,
And he and they together
Knelt down with angry prayers
For tamed and shabby tigers
And dancing dogs and bears
And wretched, blind pit-ponies
And little hunted hares.

Ralph Hodgson (1871–1962)

Contents

Introduction

Planning this book, seeking out likely contributors and collating their stories has proved an unique and rewarding experience. We are grateful to all those who wrote specially for us, to all those whom we were privileged to interview and to those who kindly gave us permission to quote from already published works. Thanks are also due to the publishers concerned, who, because all royalties are to benefit a registered Charity, kindly waived permission fees.

One surprising outcome of our meetings has been the discovery of unusual and unsuspected interests in the animal world – the international opera star who breeds Arab horses on her Sussex farm, the Member of Parliament who exercises the Queen's horses, the famous actress who is an authority on British butterflies and the law court official who races huskies.

We have sought to present a variety of views on many species, both wild and domestic, through the medium of widely differing relationships. Some contributors have hilarious stories to tell, some thought-provoking ones, but all share a love and understanding of animals and the essential part which they play in our society. We hope the book will provide an opportunity to learn more about animals – and, perhaps, about ourselves, too.

Bill and Marta Annett

Foreword

This is a most unusual book, for although there is, happily, no shortage of books about animals, this one approaches that vast subject from an original angle.

We can enjoy the opinions and experiences of a wide variety of people whose individual views on the role of the animal in society differ according to their personal involvement, inclination and idiosyncracy. Pet owners, show jumpers, wildlife conservationists, breeders, vets and zoo keepers all have fascinating things to say, not only about animals but also about humans and their attitudes – sometimes curiously insensitive – towards them.

The book is both serious and lighthearted and contains something of interest for everybody. We visit the Rothschild giraffes in Kenya, the tame foxes in the New Forest, the birds that herald the spring in the Essex countryside and the many aspects of the domestic animal, to say nothing of the hand-reared marmosets in Norfolk. On the darker side of man's stewardship of the Earth, we learn of the danger to many species of wildlife which we, as individuals, have grown up to take for granted and to love, as part of our heritage.

One aspect of our relationship with animals that is widely shared by all 'animal people' is a loathing of the use of live animals in experimentation; all the contributors have given their time and effort to support the cause in aid of which the book has been compiled.

The royalties from sales will be paid direct by the publishers to the Fund for the Replacement of Animals in Medical

Experiments. FRAME is a registered Charity, a scientific organisation devoted to the discovery and application of alternative methods in drug research and toxicity testing. A short article by the Chairman of Trustees on the work of FRAME follows this foreword.

It is recognised that over the past century live animal experimentation has played a significant part in improving medication and the safety of consumer products, not only in the interests of the human race but also of animals themselves. As Honorary President of the Animal Diseases Research Association in Edinburgh, I am well aware of the value of animal medicines and am glad to say there is much common ground in the outlook of the officials of ADRA and of the FRAME Trustees. We all share the belief that the road towards animal-free laboratories lies in the steady development of viable non-animal alternatives.

May I wish this book every success – in providing a worthwhile and enjoyable experience for readers and producing valuable funds for FRAME's important research programmes.

The Duke of Buccleuch and Queensberry KT
Drumlanrig Castle
Thornhill

January 1989

FRAME
Fund for the Replacement of Animals in Medical Experiments

FRAME is a charitable Trust, controlled solely by six honorary Trustees, ably assisted by a gifted and devoted scientific and administrative staff. From our offices in Nottingham, we publish two quarterly periodicals – a newsletter (*FRAME News*) and a scientific journal (*ATLA: Alternatives To Laboratory Animals*); we coordinate a research programme on the development and validation of alternative methods, in collaboration with sixteen industrial companies and six university and industry laboratories; we organise expert committees, such as the FRAME Toxicity Committee, which produce authoritative reports; we collaborate with other organisations, notably the British Veterinary Association and the Committee for the Reform of Animal Experimentation, to produce position papers on, for example, the reform of the Cruelty to Animals Act 1876, the use of non-human primates in British laboratories, and on the chimpanzee as a laboratory animal.

Two of FRAME's greatest achievements during its first twenty years have been its contribution to the international recognition and acceptance of the Three Rs concept of alternatives (see below) and advising the British Government during the passage of the Animals (Scientific Procedures) Act 1986.

The potential of replacement alternatives and proper administration of the new Act provide an opportunity for the future achievement of our goal of eliminating the need for *any* animal experimentation. However, there is much to be done, despite the great encouragement we receive from the general public, other charities, scientists in universities and in industry, and politicians in the All Party Parliamentary Group for FRAME.

Controversy over the exploitation of animals in the name of science has raged for hundreds of years, frequently with open hostility and bitter confrontation between militant and anti-vivisectionists advocating what are now known as animal rights, and libertarian scientists pointing to the great benefits which have accrued to human beings and animals alike.

FRAME was founded in 1969 – to occupy the middle ground, to seek cooperation instead of confrontation, and to put forward positive and constructive ideas.

We believe passionately that the current scale of live animal experimentation is unacceptable and must not be allowed to continue. However, we are also forced to accept that immediate and total abolition is not possible, if medical research is to continue and the remaining diseases which lessen the length and quality of human and animal life are to be overcome, and if new consumer products, drugs and industrial and agricultural chemicals are to be produced and used as safely as possible.

FRAME is a *Three Rs* organisation, for we believe that the only way forward is by *reduction* in the numbers of animals used, through better science and better experimental design; the *refinement* of procedures necessarily employed, so that animal suffering is minimised; and, above all, through the proper development, validation and adoption of *replacement* alternative techniques.

Progress is slow and our resources are slim. We were therefore delighted when my dear friends Bill and Marta Annett offered to follow their first great success, *Winning Through*, by compiling *For the Love of Animals* to mark the beginning of FRAME's twenty-first anniversary appeal.

Many of the contributors to *For the Love of Animals* are already long-standing friends of FRAME. Others who had known less about our efforts were pleased to be able to offer their support. What shines through their stories is that relationships with animals of all kinds greatly enrich the quality of our lives, so we should be more grateful, more considerate, and more aware of their needs.

This is completely in accord with FRAME's philosophy. We do not pretend that the issues we address are uncomplicated and that conflicts of interest can always be avoided. However, we regret the suggestion that, in facing up to the dilemma of animal experimentation we can only be *either* for humans *or* for animals. FRAME is equally committed to animal *and human* welfare.

Michael Balls MA D.Phil
Chairman of the Trustees of FRAME
and Reader in Medical Cell Biology,
University of Nottingham Medical School

1
FAMILY FRIENDS
An interview with David Amess MP

A former member of Redbridge Council, David Amess was elected to Parliament as Member for the constituency of Basildon, Essex, in June 1983. Married, with three young children, he is anxious for his family to develop the love of animals which he himself inherited from his father and which he considers essential to playing a full part in society.

Here David Amess discusses his views and how they relate to his public life.

I am a firm believer in family pets. Animals can have a very beneficial effect in teaching children the value of kindness to others and to appreciate the love which comes in return. However, there are rules to be observed if keeping a pet is to be a successful operation.

First, there is the choice of animal. My own love of animals started in early childhood, under the influence of my father, who bred budgerigars and canaries, but my enthusiasm unfortunately went beyond the bounds of reason, to the dismay of my poor mother. At school I was recognised as being animal-mad and was always allotted the task of looking after any animal used by the school in the course of education. My mother never knew what I would bring home next; it could be a rabbit, a guinea pig, a duck, and from time to time I kept lizards, a peacock and even an alligator. My parents were very understanding – they had to be!

It is generally agreed, and borne out by the evidence, that the most suitable pet for the whole family is a dog. I like cats, but I do not feel their independent nature contributes enough to the family spirit in the same way that a dog does. Small animals, such as hamsters, can be very attractive to children, but they have extremely short lives. I still remember vividly my anguish when my first hamster died at the age of eighteen months. A kindly neighbour took me to the pet shop to buy another one, but nobody explained to me that they did not live for ever and after another two years I felt I was let down again when that one died.

The second rule, devised from personal experience, is to avoid having a domestic pet when you first get married. We now have three small children, but before we started our family we had two dogs. Sarah was a crossbred golden labrador which I purchased from a pet shop for my wife's birthday and Ben was a Heinz 57 terrier – very uncertain ancestry but a really beautiful dog.

All was well until we had our first baby, when Sarah became jealous. She could not understand that she must now share our attention not only with Ben, but with a new intruder, and this she bitterly resented. So much so, that we felt she might harm the baby. It happened that some relatives had recently lost their own well-loved dog through old age and were delighted to give a home to Sarah, whom they knew well. The transfer was a great success.

Then Ben began to show signs of disturbance. He would suddenly decide to 'go walkies' on his own and disappear for hours at a time. My poor wife was constantly worried, thinking he might have been run over, and finally we had to accept an invitation from my cousin to take him. We have since tried keeping doves. I have a dovecot, and these birds are both beautiful and delightful to study. Unfortunately, they bred so fast that we could not cope with the responsibility. We have now settled, for the time being, for goldfish in our garden pond.

We shall have no more family pets until our children have all reached the age when we can introduce a dog into a complete and fully established family.

In my adult life I have been privileged to put my enthusiasm for animals to good use. A few years ago constituents came to me complaining that horses, ponies and donkeys were being dumped on wasteland in the Basildon area, which I represent, and in other parts of Essex, and there was evidence that gypsies were treating them cruelly. Reports had been received by the police and the local authority that in the small hours of the night a van would appear and take them away. Nobody could ever trace the culprits, but it was assumed that the poor creatures ended up as horse meat and were perhaps even transported abroad, and I was asked to do something about it.

This appeal resulted in my presenting to Parliament a Private Member's Bill for the protection of these animals, by providing strict rules governing tethering conditions. It was my good fortune not only that it passed its Second Reading in the Commons unanimously; in the House of Lords it was presented by Lord Houghton of Sowerby, a lifelong champion of animals, and there it was amended to widen its application. It passed into law as the Protection against Cruel Tethering Act, 1988. It is now unlawful to tether animals without specified means of tethering and the provision of water, and I am proud to have made this small contribution to animal welfare.

The encouragement of my Parliamentary colleagues was matched by the enthusiasm of the people of Basildon, who have set up a sanctuary in Wat Tyler Park, which I opened in 1987. Volunteers rallied together and raised money, and transformed a former breaker's yard into beautiful stables, in which they have now rehoused rescued horses. Basildon Zoo, which previously had some public criticism, is now under new ownership, and much hard work is being put into refurbishing the enclosures and generally improving the conditions. I am also trying to help a lady who wishes to set up a home for cats, but this is presenting a problem with the occupants of neighbouring houses!

Our schools are involved in the campaign to improve the treatment and appreciation of animals, and the constituency as a whole contains many, many people who are concerned to protect wildlife habitat.

Despite the plans my wife and I have made, the children

are already beginning to ask for guinea pigs and rabbits. They do not, of course, understand the problems these species pose with their fast-breeding habits. For myself, I am considering a compromise – tropical fish, which are very relaxing, and if I can persuade my wife, I would really love a singing canary.

2
THE GENTLE FOX
An interview with Eric Ashby

Described by Sir Peter Scott as 'the silent watcher', Eric Ashby has devoted his life to the presentation of wildlife on film, as a means of showing the true nature of our wild animals. His understanding of natural history, his patience and his acknowledged supremacy as a photographer have ensured a lasting reputation and the admiration of all animal lovers.

Eric and Eileen Ashby live in a cottage in the New Forest, and are hosts to foxes, badgers and visiting herds of fallow deer. Here he talks about them, and the menace which threatens their future existence.

I am a naturalist and my first interest is in wildlife. Photography comes second, as a useful tool in recording what I observe and as a means of conveying true pictures of our wild animals through the medium of television and film.

My first pictures, at the age of fifteen, were simple, such as studies of young birds in their nests, but I soon realised that a cine-camera gave more positive results and I saved up to buy one. I sold my still pictures and wrote an article in *Boys' Own Paper*, extolling the virtues of nature photography as an ideal hobby for boys and finally saved the £6 10s. needed for my 16 mm Ensign.

After the war I came to live here in the New Forest and began to film deer and, through a friend, my work was made known to the BBC Natural History Unit. From then on I collaborated in the making of nature films and regularly contributed to the 'Look' series and other television presentations, including *The Unknown Forest*, which was a major film about the wild mammals of the New Forest. Fallow deer, foxes and badgers were the main actors, supported by squirrels and a variety of birds in all seasons of the year. It revealed an aspect of forest life quite unknown to the tourists and holiday-makers who visit the New Forest each summer.

I have always loved the Forest and its denizens and I am very sad that man is so insensitive to the many wonderful creatures whose home it is. Take the ponies, for instance, about which I have very strong feelings. Before the war they were hardy creatures which could happily graze the gorse – a nutritious food – during the winter, and stay in first-class condition. Some would have moustaches and beards to protect them against the harshness of the gorse. Today many ponies are in bad condition and the RSPCA is currently investigating this. However, the answer is plain. For many years the ponies have been crossbred with the less hardy Arab strain to produce better riding stock – a commercial rather than ethical consideration. The result has been a deterioration in condition for these out-in-all-weather animals who have to eke out a living on poor soil. Now the demand has fallen and most of them are sold for meat, both here and abroad.

New residents in the Forest often fail to come to terms with the fact that deer will naturally roam through their gardens. I believe estate agents should emphasise the deer situation to prospective buyers, who should learn to live with these four-legged inhabitants whose rightful home the Forest is. If people object to their roses being eaten, they have the option of fencing off their gardens.

Foxes and their treatment are our special concern. They have a very bad public image, which is not their fault. From childhood, through the medium of nursery rhymes, people are conditioned to believe the fox to be a bad lot, and dirty and smelly as well. This is all quite untrue. The fox is among the cleanest and most attractive of animals and is far more gentle than the average domestic dog. In recent years we have set out to demonstrate this by playing host to rescued foxes, and visitors are delighted and astounded to find they can play with the foxes and stroke them.

It all began when we were asked to look after a three-month-old cub called Tiger, while the owners went on holiday. We kept him in the house and he was very clean and easily house-trained. When the owners decided they could not take him back, we offered to keep him. He could not, of course, remain in the house as he grew, so we built a large grass pen in our garden, where he could be kept safe until the end of the hunting season.

While the pen was being built – a month – plaster was being torn from the walls of the cottage and floor covering scratched by sharp growing claws. We began to learn a lot about foxes at close quarters!

The next step was to give him companions of his own kind and we obtained two further cubs from the RSPCA to live in the pen with him. Soon afterwards we were asked to take in an eighteen-month-old vixen named Sheba, rescued as a tiny cub after nearly drowning in a river and reared on a bottle. She was very tame and loved human company, but because she was unfamiliar with her own kind, she was afraid of the three cubs. So we added a second run, with a connecting pophole which was closed at night in order to give Sheba proper undisturbed sleep (the cubs were all nocturnal, while Sheba is diurnal and sleeps mainly at night). The four foxes now had comfortable poultry houses with covered boxes inside, filled with dry grass, but often even during a hard frost they would prefer to sleep curled up on the frozen ground.

When spring came, we offered them their freedom – all except Sheba, who could never survive in the wild. Two days later Tiger reappeared at our back door, and after that he would turn up every day to help me in the garden and play with Sheba. He would also play with our cat and with the fallow deer when they were near the cottage. One night at 11.30 p.m. I opened the back door and in came Tiger. It was six months since he had been in the cottage, but he went straight upstairs to the mat on which he had slept as a cub. At 4 a.m. I found him still asleep and deemed it wise to let him out.

We were worried about the start of the cub-hunting season

in August, and one morning in September, after hearing hounds in full cry less than a mile away, we heard that a dog fox had been killed by a car. It must have been Tiger, for once oblivious of the traffic danger, for we never saw him again.

Sheba fretted terribly and for several days refused food. She changed character and lost her happy nature; but the following spring saw an improvement, when we were given two young cubs, Jack and Jill, who had been unearthed by a bulldozer. Shortly afterwards, Sheba adopted them. She is now happy again.

Our latest guest, Wendy, has only been with us a short time, but we now have six separate runs and all the foxes are happy and welcome visitors. It is a privilege to be able to present these delightful creatures to our friends and to nature lovers who arrive from all over the country, and we hope our endeavours will do something to revise the public image of the much maligned fox.

Deer, foxes, badgers and hares all have to cope with the menace of the three organised hunts. In the New Forest there are no less than 163 meets each year and it is almost impossible to obtain any restrictions on their activities. We have pleaded in vain for our land and badger setts to be out of bounds. Our foxes, due to our care, are safe enough so long as we are here, and we dare not go out on hunting days.

We used to be happy living here among the wild animals, but this is no longer so. We now live in a state of armed defence, with alarm systems on the house, the garage and the fox pens; a sad comment on our society.

But it is our nature to be optimistic, and we now hear there is the possibility that the foxhunt will enforce a no-go area around our sanctuary, which, if effective, will be a great relief.

3
A NARROW ESCAPE
John Aspinall

A strong regard for animals, which began in John Aspinall's childhood, developed into a determination to devote his life's energies and his financial resources to the preservation of endangered species. His wild-life parks in Kent – Howletts, outside Canterbury, and Port Lympne, near Hythe – house breeding colonies of many species, from tigers, gorillas and rhinos to wild boar, antelopes and Przewalski's horses from Mongolia.

John Aspinall believes in the right of all animate beings to exist as they have always existed, and that Man has no just claim to the sanctity of human life at the expense of the animal world. However, the upholding of powerful beliefs which conflict with the convenience of human society entails calculated risks, as shown in this dramatic episode from John Aspinall's book, The Best of Friends.

I suppose that it is quite possible that I shall be killed by a wild animal. Sooner or later, with the passage of years, as the reflexes slacken and coordinative movements become more difficult, so the chances of an accident must increase.

In the autumn of 1959, I had my narrowest escape from death. It was my habit at the time to enter the large enclosure where I kept the two Himalayan bears, Esau and Ayesha. The animals were in their fourth year and were approaching adulthood. I had never had any real problems with them, though their play was so rough that I had double-thickness twill trousers made specially for their company and along with them, a heavy leather coat to protect me from their non-retractile claws. I had known the bears from infancy and had made a regular habit of jousting with them and joining in their games. One of their favourite activities was to suck my neck and to do this they had to climb up on me to reach it. If they attempted this simultaneously I usually collapsed under their weight. It was quite difficult then to extricate myself from their embrace once they had got going and I simply had to wait until they had had enough, which often took half an hour or more.

One afternoon, as was my wont, I decided to dress up and go and play with Esau and Ayesha. I took the precaution of putting on my cumbersome clothes and a heavy pair of ankle-length boots. When I arrived at their enclosure, which was surrounded by a ten-foot ha-ha ditch, I found that I had forgotten to bring the key. It was here that I made a grave error. I jumped into the pit – an easy task as the bank sloped away at an angle of forty-five degrees. I reckoned that I could shout to somebody when I wished to get out, as the area was adjacent to the main drive. Things immediately took a tricky turn. Esau was trying to copulate with Ayesha and she was not allowing him to mount properly. Each time he rose for a fresh effort, she rained blows on his head. I watched these proceedings from a distance of about thirty yards, not wanting, of course, to disturb them in any way. Esau finally looked at me after one of his abortive attempts and charged outright. I knew immediately that he meant business as he unleashed a series of frightful roars. The roar of an enraged bear is just as impressive as that of a lion, and has a nasal rather than a guttural tone. Esau fortunately was fat and unfit, whereas in those days I was in fair condition. There were three oak trees in the enclosure and I darted from one to the other in an attempt to exhaust him. I thought at first that his anger would abate in a few minutes, but this was far from the case. I was badly hampered by my heavy clothing but was reluctant to discard any of it as I thought it might prove to be some protection in the event of a clinch. However, he got so close to me in one of his rushes that I hurled my coat at him hoping it would distract him. This ruse certainly gave me some respite, as he wasted several minutes tearing it to shreds. I did not view the spectacle with much relish, however, and having satisfied himself that there was no more life left in it, the bear once again hurled himself in my direction. With every outgoing breath I was now shouting for help, but no one was in sight or apparently in hearing. My stamina seemed to be ebbing, and then, unwittingly, Ayesha came to my aid. Esau ran past her, snorting and roaring, and she turned on him thinking, no doubt, that she herself was the object of his aggression.

During this welcome interlude I decided to try and jump out of the enclosure. I took a twenty-yard run and jumped for all I was worth. I landed on the concrete wall with my elbows level with my shoulders. Under normal conditions I could easily have hauled myself out from this position, but sheer fatigue was my undoing. I slowly sank to the bottom of the ditch. In my despair I decided to lie low and hope that Esau had forgotten about me – out of sight, out of mind. I gathered a few large flint-stones and prepared myself for his arrival. A minute or so later he put in his appearance, weaving about above me, his eyes red with hatred. Luckily a bear likes to climb down a tree or a bank backwards. In an attack situation this puts him at a disadvantage and after one or two half-hearted attempts to lower himself down the bank, bottom first, he appeared to give up. I was no longer shouting, to conserve my energy for the final battle and also because I knew now that I was unlikely to be heard. After a puzzled look, Esau bundled off to the sloping path that led down to his sleeping den and adjoined the ditch. When I saw him coming towards me slowly and deliberately, I knew that he meant to settle the issue. I flung a rock at him and shouted his name with as commanding a tone as I could muster, hoping to revive in him some vestigial respect for his foster-father. He halted when the rock struck him, pained at my shouts, and then came steadily on. I remember at the time giving myself a twenty-to-one chance of survival. I was determined to die fighting, a crude flint in either hand.

In my mother-in-law's cottage meanwhile, she and a friend of mine called Richard Parkes had begun their tea. Dorothy

Hastings had heard Esau's roaring and merely thought that he was involved in a fracas with Ayesha. They were so persistent, however, that she eventually went to the back door, which was only one hundred yards from the bear pit, to try and determine what was afoot. She then heard my weakened cries and accompanied by the massive figure of Parkes, who weighed eighteen stone, and armed with saucepans and dustbin lids, they both converged on the scene of the battle. I heard them coming when Esau was about six feet from me. He pricked up his ears and fled, frightened by the sound and bustle.

They dragged me out and for an hour I sobbed while I clasped their hands. I could scarcely believe my good fortune. When it mattered, luck had been on my side.

From start to finish the whole incident probably only lasted about fifteen minutes, but to me it seemed an age. Why had Esau attacked me? The frustration of an unrequited love bound up, I suppose, with hierarchical ambitions. Either way, I never went in with him again as I thought that my ignominious flight would have convinced him of his superiority over me. I had lost face before him. Sadly, the bears never bred successfully and a few years later I sent them to Austria, as I needed their enclosure for a family of Siberian tigers.

4
EXOTIC PETS
An interview with Tony Banks MP

Tony Banks held a number of public appointments before being elected Member of Parliament for Newham North West in 1983. A former Head of Research in the AUEW and Political Adviser to the Minister for Overseas Development, he was Assistant General Secretary to the Association of Broadcasting and Allied Staff from 1976 to 1983. He was also a member of the GLC for many years and its Chairman from 1985 to 1986. Tony Banks is now Chairman of the London group of Labour MPs.

For twenty years I looked after an African grey parrot called Chunky. My father purchased her as a fledgling when he was working in the High Commission in Nigeria, and after subsequent postings, necessitating periods in quarantine, he decided that Chunky should remain in London in my care. She died in January 1988 and left a sad gap in the lives of my wife Sally and myself.

A parrot can be a source of absorbing interest. Chunky used to speak in my voice and it was hard to believe that she did not understand the word sounds she was imitating. It is accepted that the parrot's pronouncements are the result of matching particular sounds with associated actions. One amusing example of this was that every time I approached my wife to greet her, Chunky would emit kissing sounds. This we greatly enjoyed – and so did our friends!

At night we would cover the parrot cage with a cloth, from underneath which would emerge a solemn 'Good night', and in the morning, when the cloth was removed on coming down to breakfast, we were always treated to a cheery 'Good morning!' This was a very welcome start to the day.

Other associated remarks were also entertaining. If a peanut was accidentally dropped from her mouth on to the floor, Chunky would cry 'Whoops!' and an empty food bowl would bring forth the complaint 'Where's me chop? I'm starving!' She also loved loud noises and any household noise – washing up or vacuum cleaning for instance, would be doubled by the parrot rushing up and down with her contribution. The hilarious incidents would fill a book, but I remember one very funny occasion. A plumber had called to make adjustments to our central heating boiler which was housed in the basement immediately below Chunky's cage, to ensure maximum warmth for her. He began to whistle as he worked and was soon surprised to hear an echo coming from above. However he might vary the tune or the speed, it was copied, and we were sitting upstairs entranced by all this. Finally I decided it was time for an explanation and I went down to see the plumber. Just as well, as he was beginning to think one of us was making fun of him.

I did not replace Chunky when she died, as I believe it is wrong to import exotic birds and animals. I inherited my parrot for reasons already explained, but I would never purchase one, unless it had been bred in this country. The majority of exotic birds imported into the United Kingdom die, either during transportation or within a short time of arrival and it is not seemly to cause the death of living creatures in this way.

The only pet I now have is my tortoise, Snotty, which I have had for fifteen years. Another exotic species, their importation has now thankfully been banned by the EEC, but previously up to 90% would die within twelve months of arrival, through lack of understanding of their needs. Also, the method of transportation was inhumane. They came packed in wicker baskets, to give them air, but the baskets were piled high upon one another, packed six deep. All animals tend to defecate when travelling, as they become nervous, and the tortoises in the bottom baskets would be suffocated.

Those who survived and were sold as family pets suffered through having to exist in an unfriendly climate without due care and attention. If a pet is not a natural inhabitant of this country, study should be made of its background and the climate of its country of origin. For instance, to let a tortoise remain outside in the garden throughout the winter, is frequently fatal. Personally, I do not favour letting a tortoise hibernate at all. They do not choose to sleep through the winter for any reason other than instinct. They are endothermic; that is to say, they are cold-blooded and derive their energy from heat absorbed from outside. Thus, nature tells them that winter is coming, with its shortage of food and lack of heat, and their defence is to go to sleep, in order to expend minimum energy, living on the reserves built up in the warmer months.

If you can make provision for winter food and heating there is no need for hibernation. I have constructed a large box in which my tortoise spends a happy, lively and comfortable winter indoors. Lined with newspaper (they tend to defecate every other day) and properly fed, Snotty enjoys the warmth of a heat lamp, which is on a timer and operates accordingly. Admittedly, her exercise area is restricted, but that does not seem to bother her unduly and she eagerly enjoys food taken from my hand. Finally, in order to keep her shell, neck and head in good condition, I rub a little olive oil on her.

In the summer she lives in the garden, but here again I take good care of her. I have converted a tea chest into a weatherproof home and I supplement the food she gets from the garden with cereals and other things she likes.

It is the responsibility of all who choose to keep pets to preserve them. Once a species is extinct, it cannot be recreated by man and this responsibility covers all wild animals. Politicians have a special duty in this respect, as it is they who make the laws governing the treatment and protection of animal life and define the penalties to be imposed upon those who contravene them.

We have to remember that the world does not belong to us. We are fortunate to be living in it at this time and we have a duty to pass it on to our children in as healthy a state, if not healthier, than we inherited. We disregard this at our peril.

5
MY ARAB HORSES

An interview with Josephine Barstow CBE BA

Josephine Barstow is an international opera singer. Born in Sheffield and educated at Birmingham University, she made her debut in 1964, became a Contract Principal at Sadler's Wells in 1967 and with the Welsh National Opera (1968–70), followed by many leading roles at Covent Garden and a long and fruitful relationship with the English National Opera. The year 1977 saw her debut in the United States, and she has since been singing regularly in most of the major opera houses of the world. With her husband Ande Anderson she farms in Sussex and breeds pure Arab horses. She describes her devotion to her animals and the satisfaction of maintaining two such differing life interests.

The decision to breed Arab horses brought a new dimension into my life. The schedule of an opera singer involves extensive travel, long periods away from home and family and, at times, a feeling of loneliness. A compensating major interest is essential to personal fulfilment. Some singers are keen gardeners, some take up golf, but I think I am the only one to settle on horse breeding.

I have always had an affinity with animals. I seem to know how to cope with them and they respond to me. My husband and I used to live in London, but we had a cottage in Sussex and I was able to ride when we were there. However, we decided we had got things the wrong way round, so we bought a farm which had been used for pig rearing and moved into the country. I started to collect horses and soon became interested in Arabs as there is an important stud near our home and I thought they were the most wonderful horses in the world. The decision to breed quickly followed.

Ours is a small stud at the moment, but the aim is that it should be financially viable by the time I retire from singing. This will then be my second career. So at the moment I am concentrating on building up a herd with only the highest possible quality breeding stock. Breeding is a fascinating exercise. I have to get to know my mares intimately, study their pedigrees and match them against that of the sire. Every time I think I have got it right; the two horses seem to complement each other temperamentally and physically, the pedigrees make sense and I settle down to wait for this piece of perfection that will hit the ground in eleven months' time. But, as anyone who deals with animals – especially horses – knows, they have an amazing habit of regularly proving one wrong. Of course, whatever the level of perfection, each baby enchants me within the first minutes of my acquaintance and I am enslaved and involved again. Arabitis is a terminal disease!

The fascination of breeding is complex; one is involved emotionally because one loves the mares. The ramifications of trying to get the genetics right are an exercise for the most complex of brains. Flair and an artistic eye are also needed, to grasp the essentials of each horse conformationally and to be able to see clearly where improvements could be made. However, the artistic and emotional satisfaction of watching a group of Arab horses at liberty and at play in a field is a reward richer than anyone could hope for.

The birth of my first Arab foal was one of the most precious experiences of my life. It was February and snow was falling. The night was still and silent except for the almost inaudible dry sound of snowflakes landing on already fallen snow. This was my mare's first foal and also my own first experience of birth, but there was no fear, more a feeling of the rightness of things. The foal's tiny front feet were already showing as the mare lay down, and I knelt behind her to help if she needed me. With one big effort she very quickly had his head and shoulders and most of him in the world, and we settled back to wait while they both rested. When the foal moved and broke the cord to his mother, I eased him away from her and carried him round for her to see. She raised herself up on to her elbow to look at him in surprise and wonder; he just looked back, ears pricked, intelligence already showing in his eye. The moment was one of utmost peace.

I am always astonished at how meticulous nature is in her arrangements for life. Foals come exquisitely packaged even to little pads of jelly on their feet so that they don't damage their mother on the journey out into the world. I never leave them till they have had their first good drink and sometimes this takes a while; the colt foals especially seem to take much longer to get the hang of this first lesson. I love working with the babies; one can start training very early – at two to three days – by putting on a head collar. The early handling is so important.

Last year my husband and I went to Jordan to a festival of Arabian horses, known as the Arabian Horse at Home. It was hosted by Princess Alliya, the daughter of King Hussein of Jordan, and breeders from most of the Arab countries brought their horses and showed them. There were horses from Bahrein, Saudi Arabia, Egypt and Iraq, and it was fascinating to see how the Arabs really care for them. We went off into the desert, sightseeing, and we could imagine how the Bedouins used to live – a way of life now rapidly disappearing. For centuries the horse was their currency and the mares were their most treasured possessions. The Arabs have some wonderful sayings, like 'Every Arabian mare's belly is a treasure chest of gold'. This always crosses my mind when I go out into the field and see all my treasure chests!

Animals are wonderful friends as they have qualities which we humans have lost. They seem to have a short cut to what I call the mystery of life. Cats in particular have it, and so do horses; I think that is why I enjoy their company. Horses have a special kind of grace that makes me feel privileged to be allowed into their lives. I am giving them the basic necessities of life, but they are giving me something far more precious and impossible to describe. Moreover, such powerful creatures could seriously hurt you, but they go out of their way to avoid harming you. If you treat them well, they repay you a thousandfold and give you their services without question.

I thoroughly enjoy my singing career and value tremendously the satisfaction it brings. Far from interfering with that side of my life, the horses have provided a cushion, a balance, so that should an opera performance be disappointing, it is not the end of the world. In this way, indeed, I have become more detached in my attitude to my career and I believe this has helped me to improve my performances.

The stud is also a wonderful project to share with my husband and family; we are building something together and are bound together by it. Even the long separations made inevitable by my singing are somehow easier to bear, and endless equine discussions take place over the international telephone services. I am extremely lucky. There comes a time in the life of every singer when it is prudent to bring one's career to a close. I love my work, but when I have to give it up I shall have the joy of knowing I can give all my time to my Arab horses.

6
SPRINGER SPANIELS
An interview with The Duchess of Beaufort

The Duchess of Beaufort is the daughter of the Marquess of Bath and is married to the 11th Duke. Badminton, their home, is host to the famous horse trials and they are both ardent lovers of animals. The Duchess talked to us about her dogs and other animals which play a significant part in life at Badminton.

I have always had dogs, right from childhood. The first dog in my life was a bulldog called Emerald, and after her came a Shetland sheepdog whom I loved dearly. Sadly, he was run over. Then came a corgi, which I did not like overmuch, but that was followed by dachshunds and one particular wire-haired called Janet. These I liked very much. I find that dogs are like people – there are some you take to and some you don't.

Now I have two springer spaniels, Mabel and Lottie. I am devoted and wedded to them and will always have springers now, but I would never advise anyone else to have them. They are essentially gun dogs and they are by no means suitable as house dogs. They are very excitable and highly strung and they need a lot of exercise and attention.

Mabel and Lottie are from the same litter and are now seven years old. We wanted a dog and had previously bought a springer for one of my sons. He was the father of Lottie and Mabel, and that was how we chose Mabel. However, we were asked to look after Lottie temporarily, for the person who had booked her was abroad at the time. But, of course, after six weeks we couldn't bear to hand her over, so we kept them both, rather to the annoyance of the person who was expecting to collect her. We originally called her Spot, as she has a dark spot on her head, but then my husband said we couldn't possibly call her that, it was like calling her Boil, so we tried Spotty and several other alternatives and eventually settled on Lottie, a name she found it easy to answer to.

Although they are twins, the two dogs have completely different characters. Mabel is extremely aggressive, while Lottie is content to take a back seat and let her sister do the shouting. They like visitors once they are in the house, but getting past the door is always a problem. When the bell rings, they bark – and Mabel is all prepared for the attack. Lottie stays in the background and cheers her on with loud barks. There have been occasions when guests have had a nasty bite from Mabel. And there are no half measures with her. She does not just nip at the ankles; she jumps up and bites the upper arm. I'm afraid there has been many a tetanus injection, and even stitches, for some of my guests. It can be quite an expensive business, paying doctor's bills for injured visitors!

Once the weekend guests have arrived, they can then come in and out without danger, but if they come a second time, they have to be reintroduced. It's quite a worry, but I am grateful at other times for their protection. For instance, last year we had an attempted burglary. One night, at half-past one in the morning, the burglar alarm went off. This it does fairly frequently and at first I thought it was the usual false alarm. However, the alarm indicates where the trouble is and this was apparently in the library, which aroused my suspicions. My husband was away, so Mabel and Lottie and I went along – and then Mabel suddenly flew at somebody in the dark. Lottie said, 'Oh well, that's that. I think I shall go back to bed', and retired immediately. Mabel, however, attacked the man and made him drop the bag in which were the things he was intending to steal. I didn't actually see him, but I heard the kerfuffle with Mabel. He quickly fled, the way he had entered, before I would turn on the light.

I was very grateful to Mabel and very proud of her. She was very puzzled because we were praising her for something for which she was normally whacked! This incident attracted considerable publicity in the media, not only over here but also in New York, where my youngest son now lives. He rang the next day to say he had read in the New York papers about Mabel, the Wonder Dog! It was quite an exhilarating experience but one I would not wish to be repeated. My one regret is that the burglar omitted to leave his card in the swagbag.

Lottie is very good with children. Mabel has not bitten any severely but she has given them a nip sometimes, so children are not allowed to touch her. When she sees children making a fuss of Lottie, she looks at her as if to say, 'All you have to do is to give them a little nip and they won't be allowed to touch you.' Both dogs are very happy when we have visitors, and when I have groups coming to see round the house, they adopt a proprietorial air and enjoy taking them from room to room.

At Badminton we have many animals. Horses galore, of course, and a herd of deer. The keeper has one tame deer which was deserted by its mother. He fed it from a bottle and now it thinks it's a dog and won't leave him. It won't mix with other deer and it's a bit of a worry now, because it is a male and when the rutting season comes, it will be looking for a mate and will start getting a bit stroppy. At the moment he's no trouble. He comes into the house and the dogs don't seem to mind. They adopt an attitude of tolerance. He came into the hall the other day, when the daily ladies were polishing the floor. He started nudging them, and when they remonstrated he began slipping all over the freshly polished floor. He's very tame indeed. It's just a pity it wasn't a hind; that would have been far less complicated.

At one time the late Duke and Duchess had fourteen dogs, mostly terriers, and they all had the run of the house. My girls are not allowed on any chairs except one special lot which they regard as their own, but the terriers were allowed to sit anywhere, and did. I remember guests being invited to sit down, but when confronted with bared teeth and an ominous growl, they would say 'No, thanks – I like standing!'

Mary, the late Duchess, had a badger for years. It was

totally tame; she took it for walks and people could stroke it. There were amusing moments when some gracious lady who had come to tea suddenly became aware of something moving around under her skirt! However, one mating season the Duchess put her outside – there was a male badger in the grounds. She fed her for three days, and after that the badger disappeared. We all hoped it was a happy love match.

I am not very keen on parrots, and the late Duchess left us with the responsibility for hers. They bit people without any warning and one of them once bit Prince Charles quite badly. It drew blood, and that drop of blue blood went to the parrot's head and he proceeded to bite everyone in sight. On another occasion I was having a charity party and I put up a large notice saying *Do not touch this parrot. It bites.* However, the parrot ate the notice and bit everyone!

All animals are wonderful creatures and warrant our protection and respect. To me, however, dogs are very special and quite unique as companions.

7
DOLPHINS AND DOGS
An interview with Andrew Bowden MBE MP

Member of Parliament for Brighton Kemptown since 1970, Andrew Bowden is National President of the Captive Animals Protection Society, a member of the Parliamentary Animal Welfare Group and a member of the National Advisory Panel of PRO-DOGS. As well as his commitment to the welfare of animals, Andrew Bowden is also Joint Chairman of the All Party Parliamentary Group for Pensioners and Chairman of the Parliamentary Group for British Limbless Ex-Servicemen, a member of Ardingly College School Council and a Fellow of the Industry and Parliament Trust. He is also a member of the Council of Europe. He is married with one son and one daughter.

The life of a Member of Parliament is demanding enough, without the addition of self-imposed responsibilities; but when animals are involved, there is no choice other than to play an active part to protect them from cruelty and abuse.

My family and I live in a flat in Brighton with seventy-two stairs and no lift. I leave home after breakfast and hope to return by midnight on working days, and nobody would normally plan to add the responsibility of household dogs to such a lifestyle. However, we have three West Highland terriers and I owe my physical fitness to their demands and needs.

I have always had a deep love and concern for all animals, and it was with regret that my wife and I originally decided, logically, that we could not have a pet. An animal becomes part of the family, and time must be found to treat it properly. Fate, however, had other ideas. An elderly resident in the house had a West Highland terrier bitch, Tammie, whom we frequently exercised, and one day she decided she could no longer cope and Tammie must be put down. Tammie was a friend and there was no question of a one-way ticket to the vet, so we adopted her.

Unfortunately, Tammie's early upbringing had left its mark. Terriers are apt to be unpredictable in any case, but can be more than usually difficult if not properly disciplined early on. A local vet whom we consulted suggested we allowed Tammie to have some pups, which might settle her down. Great preparations were made; the dining room was converted into a delivery room and thoroughly sanitised, and every provision was made for the expected new arrivals. At three o'clock one morning the first of three pups arrived. The vet was called and supervised the delivery of the other two.

The agreed policy was to find good homes for two of the pups and keep one as company for Tammie. One went, at the proper time, to a bank manager in Lewes, but very soon we became so attached to the remaining dog that we could not part with him. And that is how a busy MP and his wife, living in a top floor flat, have three West Highland terriers – mother, son and daughter.

We now have a car specially adapted to take an argumentative mother in one compartment and two eager children in another, and every morning, come rain, wind or snow, either my wife or I take them for an hour of exercise at 6 a.m. With regular shorter walks during the day, too, they are happy and fit – and so are their owners!

At weekends the dogs accompany us to various engagements, and on one occasion they created quite a diversion at a church service for animals. We had two of our dogs with us, and their behaviour was impeccable until just before the end of the service. A lady in an adjoining pew had brought a cat in a basket. During the final prayer, Tibbles managed to unlatch the lid. She made for home down the centre aisle, closely followed by two barking West Highland terriers resolutely ignoring the frantic cries of an impotent master. The incident caused quite a stir among the congregation, who were no doubt confused by the names of the dogs; they are regis-

tered with the Kennel Club as Tammie Hansard, Ben Hansard
and Speaker Hansard. I wisely find I do not recall which two
participated in the church performance!

Loving and caring for family pets is very rewarding, but
that does not necessarily constitute a love of animals. I think
that if one is properly concerned with the animal world then
much more is required. In Parliament I am a member of the
Parliamentary Animal Welfare Group, which covers all aspects
of the subject, but my particular concern is for captive animals, animals which are taken away from their natural
environment to entertain human beings. I am proud to be the
National President of the Captive Animals Protection Society,
which campaigns for the complete cessation of the use of
animals performing to human audiences. There is no justifi-
cation for magnificent animals like elephants, tigers, lions and
bears being taught pathetic little party tricks to make the
public laugh. It is not only degrading to the animals, it is
equally degrading to those who present them and those who
pay to see them.

For many years I have been personally involved with the
exploitation of dolphins. All the evidence is that the dolphin
is probably the most intelligent animal on the planet, exclud-
ing man, and sooner or later, when the breakthrough comes,
intercommunication between us will be greatly enhanced. To
take a wild dolphin out of the sea and put it in a small display
pool to perform tricks hourly for twelve hours a day is a
disgrace to the human race. It is said that in some dolphinaria
there are punishments, such as withdrawal of food, if the
animals do not act up to standard, but they must get bored
with their repetitive tasks, which are far below their mental
capacity. Imagine a group of us being captured and taken
against our will to another planet, peopled with beings far
more intelligent than ourselves. We are put in cages, housed
and fed, but made to perform tricks many times a day to
amuse these superior beings, just because our own intelligence
is limited by comparison to theirs.

I am delighted that for many years the British Government
has not allowed the importation of dolphins into this country

and I hope that when the present dolphin population has died, the dolphinarium will disappear for ever. Fortunately, dolphins do not easily breed in captivity. In the meantime we can press for improvement in conditions, such as larger pools, feeding regulations and more stringent water tests.

Dolphins and dogs – their circumstances differ greatly; but the future of all animals is in our hands, and we must take care to uphold our responsibilities.

8
WORTHY OF RESCUE
An interview with Katie Boyle

Famous as a TV and radio personality, former international model and for eighteen years 'Dear Katie' in the TV Times, *Katie Boyle is the daughter of an Italo-Russian nobleman and an Anglo-Austrian mother. A love of animals, especially unwanted and ill-treated dogs and cats, has been a priority throughout her eventful life and she is now devoting her main energies to the greater public understanding of animal needs.*

As a family we always had dogs – and nearly always they were rescued ones. I remember once counting them at our home in Italy; there were eighteen of all shapes and sizes, from Great Danes down to pekes, with a few mongrels thrown in for good measure. We had cats, too, and wherever we went we always travelled with two Siamese plus two pekes. On one occasion, when I was about eight years old, my beloved step-mother, who adored pekes, actually had six puppies delivered to the Savoy Hotel in London. We drove all the way back to Italy with them, and I still remember how beautifully behaved they were.

I was first given my very own dog when I was twelve, on the strict understanding that during the school holiday I assumed total responsibility for Suki's care and welfare. That meant feeding, exercising, grooming, bathing and generally looking after her, and I was kept to this pact by being shown how much fun and satisfaction a dog can bring.

I feel strongly that this is the best – indeed, the only proper way – to introduce children to domestic pets. But it *must* be with the enthusiastic cooperation of their parents. Pet-owning engenders in a youngster consideration not only for the animals concerned, but for people too, and makes clear the rewards which accompany responsibility.

My father felt so strongly against cruelty to animals that he was not above 'lifting' one in its best interests. Once, he brought home a beautiful black and white spaniel. He'd been in a restaurant, and couldn't understand the weird sounds coming from under the next table. Apparently, there was a dog underneath a woman's chair whose paws she trod on deliberately, and it was tethered too tightly for it to move out of her way. My father carefully approached from behind, slipped the dog's collar and left with the animal.

It was the sight of these unfortunate dogs and cats who used to appear from time to time which developed my strong feelings for them, and it was whilst watching their fear and nervousness gradually being replaced by confidence and an unbelievable devotion to us, that I realised and experienced the joy and satisfaction that rehabilitating previously ill-treated animals can bring.

When I came to live in England after the war, I hated being without a pet of my own, but it wasn't possible to have one so I thought I might prove useful to a number of lost ones in care. I got in touch with the Director of Battersea Dogs Home and offered to start a service collecting food from restaurants and delivering it to Battersea. I was quite unprepared for Commander Knight's reaction: 'I take pride in keeping our strays as fit as possible,' he said, 'and I don't want them poisoned by table scraps!' Years later, when I was invited to join the committee of the home, he and I remembered this incident and by then I had learnt how right he was.

I am very active in my relationship with the Dogs Home, and have often been out with the vans to collect stray dogs from some of the one hundred and eighty police stations in the Greater London area. We have five vans going out six days a week, and it is distressing to see at first hand how man's irresponsibility to dogs is increasing. When I first took part in this exercise, the vans used to bring back an average of four or five dogs apiece each day – now the numbers have nearly doubled.

There is a simple, but drastic, long-term solution for which I, and a great many others (amongst them some highly reputable vets), have been campaigning for years. That is to cut down dramatically on the number of registered breeders, and then to neuter and spay pet dogs, certainly all those living in our larger cities. Imagine one bitch having a litter of ten puppies today. This time next year, if each of those puppies grew up to either father or produce one litter, and assuming each have five offspring, there would be fifty new dogs. A little simple arithmetic will show that, in a total of seven years, over a quarter of a million dogs could be produced from that single unspayed bitch. It needs very little imagination to realise how many of those creatures might become latchkey dogs, or simply homeless and unwanted.

I have three rejects myself. A black toy poodle who was found wandering and bewildered in Bromley, a white scrap who was found screaming in a gutter with a broken hip by my vet, and a third, whom we call Charley-Girl. She was a scruffy little stray that I found wandering across a busy motorway on a bitterly cold February day in 1986. I reported her to a number of police stations, then took her to Battersea Dogs Home, where she was instantly recognised as having been there two or three times before. I didn't leave her there that time, and she has become an intrinsic part of my permanent trio of rescuees. I called her Charley simply because I thought she was a boy until I washed her, and then didn't like to add to her other traumas by changing her name yet again. She has turned out to be extra intelligent, kind and instinctively obedient. Though she still growls at newcomers, if she has any doubts about them, I can assure them that she won't bite – because somewhere in her previously unhappy life her teeth were filed down.

There is an ever increasing need for loving and sensible homes for healthy stray dogs taken in and cared for by sanctuaries, but they must be homes where people have an added understanding, who are prepared to 'think dog' and learn how a dog's mind really works.

Every Friday, on LBC, after my conversation piece with Steve Jones, I offer listeners an Orphan of the Day. Recently, a well-meaning lady took in a little terrier. I had warned her to let *him* decide very gradually to approach her. I added that he had been extremely badly treated and trusted nobody, and told her that he might snap. This dog had been to hell and back, and needed an owner with enormous patience and, above all, a doggy empathy. A few days later, this lady rang to say that the dog had indeed bitten her, and would we take him away. Apparently, she had left him to spend the night on the drawing room sofa, but in the early hours woke up and began to worry. She then tiptoed downstairs, went quietly into the drawing room and sat down, still in the dark, beside the dog! He suddenly woke up, couldn't make out the shape next to him and in fright flew at her. Had she put herself in the dog's place, she would have understood why. She knew that she was trustworthy, but the dog hadn't been given time enough to convince himself of this fact.

Dogs that have found their way to an animal rescue centre will have been through some pretty bewildering experiences and are decidedly uptight and wary. But, speaking personally, I know that if they are accorded very special tender loving care and are rehabilitated with a fair, firm and fun approach, laced with a special understanding, they will make the most devoted and loyal of companions. But I repeat, they *do* have to be approached in a very different way from that cuddly pup which comes straight from a contented litter.

I have already gathered a small, most experienced and knowledgeable team, and I want to devote as much time as possible in the future to promoting the understanding of these animals. I know it is going to take a lot of willing work and a public platform to put across this very simple, but essential, message. But I feel sure there are a lot of people who will be only too happy to listen and learn and build up a really satisfying relationship with their pets.

9
SHOWJUMPERS WITH HEART
An interview with David Broome OBE

The name of David Broome brings to mind champion horses such as Sunsalve, Mr Softee, Beethoven, Sportsman and Philco. Professional Champion of the world, he has also been European Champion three times, Olympic Bronze Medallist twice, and in 1981 created a record as five times winner of the King George V Gold Cup.

Coming from Welsh farming stock, David Broome also farms four hundred acres in Gwent. He is married and has three sons.

I started competitive showjumping at about the age of nine, as did my sister, Liz Edgar. We were very fortunate as the opportunity was provided for us by our family. My father and grandfather were always associated with farming and horses. My father had ridden all his life and after the war he started showjumping. He was a dedicated man, one who set great store by maximum effort and the will to win, and he was the inspiration behind it all. I believe that if you look into the history of most successful showjumping riders, you will find somebody responsible in the background.

This sport is rather complicated in that you must have all the facilities – the right horse, stabling, somewhere to practise in order to keep the horse exercised and in good fettle – and if, in addition, you have a parent who is not only dedicated but also knowledgeable, you have all the support you could wish for.

I also believe that a good home environment is a great blessing. I thoroughly enjoy being at home with my family – it provides a good contrast from the competitive life in the ring. We farm four hundred acres and we have about three hundred and fifty ewes and some cattle in addition to our horses. We also market a prepacked feed product, Horsehage, which fits in with my calendar and interest, being a product especially for horses. We mow the grass in summer, dry it for twenty-four hours and then, compressed and sealed in airtight bags, it preserves all the June goodness for the horses in winter. Farming is not by any means the most profitable way to make a living, but it is a great way of life and fits in well with showjumping.

Picking a horse is one of the trickiest stages. All horses are individuals, like people. Some are nice, but, just like humans, there are others at the opposite end who have no wish to cooperate to the full. Fortunately, these are a small percentage. I have been lucky in my long career to find some very good horses and if I were asked to name a favourite, it would have to be Sportsman. He was lovely. I found him as a four-year-old, through a friend in Ireland, and bought him as a novice. I took him through all the stages of training and nursed him through all the hiccups in his career. Many people think Sportsman was one of the nicest horses ever in showjumping. He always tried to do his best.

Countryman, my current number one horse, actually looks very much like Sportsman. He is a nine-year-old and since the beginning of the season he has greatly improved. He did me proud at the Olympics in Seoul and, for such an inexperienced horse, I was delighted with his performance. And I was lucky, too, because the jumping in Seoul suited a younger horse better than an older one. Countryman is tough but learns slowly, and it took six months to break him in. This is an unusually long time, but if you can use that side of a horse's character to your advantage, you find yourself with a horse that is all heart – and that is what matters.

My horses have to travel a great deal, and there again they all travel differently, some more calmly than others. It is essential to give them sufficient space; in a too confined area they can panic, and if that happens you have a difficult job to overcome it. Horses get very worried in claustrophobic

conditions. They flew to the Olympic Games with absolutely
first-class treatment. They had a wonderful flight and it only
took fourteen hours, as Mrs Thatcher had thoughtfully
obtained permission for the plane to fly over Russian territory.
They flew in a specially equipped horse plane carrying a large
number of horses, with plenty of room to stand with their
legs apart.

We often have problems with the air security regulations,
which stipulate that every groom should be strapped into his
seat belt on take off and landing – just the very times when
the groom should be with his horse, when they may need a
little help and reassurance. Every animal caretaker would
agree on that and I am sure they all act according to their
conscience!

I do a lot of travelling, but now I think nothing of it. At
most of the shows I attend in the winter I jump on a Sunday
afternoon and I will be back in the house by 9 p.m. the same
evening. I fly back, gaining an hour, while the staff drive the
horses either to another show for the following week or home
in the horsebox. I must admit, though, I was rather tired
when I arrived at Seoul last year. We had flown to Calgary
the previous week, had jumped there every day on different
horses, left there on Sunday night and landed back at Heathrow at 2 p.m. on the Monday afternoon. I drove home to
Wales and had to leave again at 8 a.m. the next morning to
return to Heathrow and catch the midday plane to Seoul.

Showjumping is a clean healthy sport, without any of the
unpleasant aspects of some of the team sports. All efforts are
individual, out in the open in the show ring, and there is a
spirit which contributes to general goodwill among competitors. The situation at the present time is an interesting one.
There are a number of riders in the top class who are of similar
standard – I might mention, for instance, Nick Skelton, the
Whitakers and Robert Smith – and the discovery of an exceptional horse by any one of them can make all the difference.
Management, too, plays an important part. Young, inexperienced riders do not always appreciate that and tend to plan

from day to day, whereas you should look at your horse over twelve months, or even longer.

The relationship between horse and rider is greatly influenced by the way the horse is handled in training, and I firmly believe in discipline. The stricter you are, the more obedient the horse will learn to become and a happy relationship will develop. If a naughty horse gets away with it, he will fail to see life in a positive way and will always be looking for a way to shortchange you. I have one at the moment, my third horse, who is a tricky little devil with a character quite different from my first two. He is always looking for a way out – to say 'I've had enough of this', as it were. So there are always exceptions to the rule and you just have to work harder and think quicker with these types.

I consider myself lucky. I still have the competitive spirit and enjoy what I do, but I do not need to go out in the rain and I will not jump when conditions are poor. I have had a few bad falls in my time; I had one at Hickstead a couple of years ago which took three or four days to get over, but, luckily, serious injuries in showjumping are not frequent.

As you get older you become aware that time does not stand still and you must be less ambitious. You need better horses than when you were in the twenties or thirties and I am very happy that I now have two good ones. I hope that with their cooperation I shall be able to enjoy showjumping for a long time yet.

10
ALL ANIMALS ARE EQUAL
An interview with The Very Rev. Edward Carpenter
KCVO DD

Dr Carpenter has enjoyed a distinguished career in the Church of England, culminating in his tenure as Dean of Westminster from 1974 to 1985. His interests are wide and he chairs a number of societies, besides being a member of international religious and social committees.

Author of many publications on matters of religion, Dr Carpenter is also well known and highly respected for his views on the human treatment of animals. He is married and has three sons and one daughter.

My approach to animals is an intellectual one. Of course, people are understandably and rightly fond of their pets and thus treat them with consideration and kindness. However, there should be an equal concern for animals who are not so attractive. They have an equal right to be treated with respect and consideration, although they do not appear so 'cuddly'. People are inclined to forget that and to be indifferent to the unattractive species.

Today there is much cruelty towards animals outside the home – animals which are used, and misused, for our own purposes. When I was at Westminster, a few of us got together – some with particular, specialised interests – and produced a survey under the title *Animals and Ethics*. It was an effort to look at the total range of our relationship with this order of creation, to ask questions about it and formulate a reasonable critique.

In every society you will find individuals who indulge in

cruelty, not only to animals but to their own kind as well. However, I believe the real problem today vis-à-vis animals is institutionalised violence – that is, where cruel practices are carried out by respectable people, often remote operators. In my view this covers activities such as factory farming, live animal experimentation and certain areas of the training of animals for public entertainment.

The taking of life is a serious matter. I contributed, some years ago, an article in a book published by Gollancz against the practice of hunting as a sport. I still maintain that my stance represents a Christian position. It is said that hunting is the best way to keep animal populations in check, but that is not the main point. Let us assume for a moment that certain species of animal must be kept down in numbers. Let us further assume, which I do not, that hunting is not cruel. I would still say that it is morally wrong, because to convert this into a sport – to do it for fun – is quite seriously immoral.

If ever a life is taken it should be done with reverence and in a situation which you wish did not require it. The tsetse fly bringing bubonic plague cannot be given immunity, but it is sad that this should be so; to have their destruction converted into an opportunity for fun would be wrong, in my opinion.

In the Book of Genesis we read that God gave man dominion over the animals, but this may well be interpreted in terms of stewardship – being responsible for. Anyhow, I would not rely on one isolated text. No one, surely, would wish to subscribe to the view of the psalmist, 'Blessed is he who dasheth my children against the wall'!

One of the most disturbing problems to the religious consciousness is the predatory character of nature itself – what St Paul describes as bondage. Such a state existed long before man emerged on the scene at all. Indeed, the predator has been in part the agent of evolution. Surely it is our task in this respect to transcend nature, to be cooperative and caring, stewards of the world that God has entrusted into our fallible hands. Nothing is more tragic than for it to be ruined by material greed and a misuse of near absolute power.

I remember reading a mythological book entitled *Dance of the Devil*, by the German author Gunther Schwab. It is a symbolic novel in which the Devil, having tried for centuries to destroy mankind, always finds that when on the verge of success, man fights back and reasserts himself. Finally the Devil has to admit that he is powerless to defeat man in the traditional way and decides he must contrive a way by which man destroys himself. He thus, with great subtlety, instils into the mind of man that if you have the *power* to do something, it is *right* to do it, and that any use of technological power is progress. The Devil then climbs to the top of a mountain and watches man contrive his own self-destruction.

I believe there is a lesson to be learned from this story and that a rethink of our control of the animal kingdom and nature, through our new-found power, would provide a logical start. If we are content to sit back and say there is nothing we can do about the state of the world, then we are hastening our own doom. But I believe that young people today are taking a much more progressive and optimistic view, and seeking to promote the real values which recent generations have tended to regard as secondary to material gain.

11
AN AMATEUR WHO LOVES BIRDS
by Lord Chelwood of Lewes MC DL

Lord Chelwood, who died in April 1989, was well known for his deep interest in wildlife and nature conservation. President of the Royal Society for the Protection of Birds from 1966 to 1970, he was awarded the RSPB Gold Medal. He was also a past President of the Sussex Trust for Nature Conservation and of the Sussex Downsmen, and was President-elect of the Sussex Ornithological Conservancy Council.

Educated at Stowe, Tufton Beamish joined the Royal Northumberland Fusiliers from Sandhurst in 1937, saw active service in Palestine and then fought throughout the 1939–45 war in Europe, Malaya, Burma and North Africa. He went to the Staff College in 1945 and in the same year succeeded his father as Conservative MP for Lewes, a seat he held for twenty-nine years. Knighted in 1961, he was created a Life Peer in 1974. As Deputy Leader of the first British delegation to the European Parliament he was the prime mover in setting up the Grzimek Committee, which led to the European Birds Directive. An author of considerable note, Lord Chelwood's books include two about the Soviet Union and the occupied countries in Europe, and an account of the Battle of Lewes in 1264.

'Music both amuses and soothes' said Horace Walpole. The same is true of birds; how much those miss who never notice them. They offer free, continuous entertainment and joy at home and throughout the world, from Timbuktu to Vladivostok.

Some five hundred species of birds, including 'accidentals', may be seen in Britain, so it is a luxury to visit New Zealand

or the Seychelles to see the two rarest robins in the world.
There may be more varieties to watch in one's own garden
than by climbing mountains or wading through bogs. Sharp
eyes and ears, good field glasses and a pocket guide, and there
you are.

My brother and I were lucky enough to grow up in the
Sussex countryside, with animals part of the family. Clover,
our Shetland pony, was so fat that riding her made me bandy-
legged. Dogs from Border terriers to Sealyhams, were our
constant companions in and out of bed. We spent many happy
night hours watching foxes and badgers.

Birds shared our breakfast table, and Horace, the hawfinch
with a broken wing, lived safely in a cage with us for five
years until the farm cat got him. A colony of crossbill bred in
the pines by our gate throughout the thirties. One day choughs
gave aerial displays, just like lapwing. Gilbert White claimed
he saw 200 on Beachy Head. Ours were escapees, of course.
In Blackboys, where I now live, in Guy Mountfort's former
house, our count and his together come to 131 species of
birds, of which 71 have bred. Not bad!

During and since the war I have travelled widely, and it is
one of the comical and diverting memories of birds that stay
in my mind as much as seeing an occasional rarity. In Jamaica,
a mocking bird regularly woke me early by imitating my alarm
clock. In Tobago, having crawled to bed at 3 a.m. after an
exhausting flight, the phone rang *brr! brr!* every half-hour,
despite my protests to the exchange. The culprit was a little
red-headed woodpecker on the corrugated iron roof.

In the Caroni Swamp in Trinidad, the sight of hundreds of
scarlet ibis swirling in a clear blue sky and landing on the
mangroves to make them look like brilliant Britannia rhododendrons was breathtaking. Then there were the brown peli-
cans that dived from thirty foot or bellyflopped to catch small
fish on Useppa Island off Florida. Often a tern would sit on
a pelican's head and snatch the fish from its beak. Then came
the 'Magnificent' frigate bird with its seven-foot wingspan to
mob the tern and catch the fish before it hit the water. Man
o' war indeed!

I remember with special delight seeing a dabchick on Lake Baringo in Kenya diving with three chicks on its back, a trick I fancy no other bird can perform; and the three hamerkops on Lake Malawi that displayed, croaking to each other, wings outspread. Like circus acrobats they stood on each other's backs, but when a fourth tried to get on top they all collapsed with cackles of laughter.

These are just ramblings of an amateur who loves birds and is sad that their numbers inevitably dwindle as their habitats are destroyed. Lewis Carroll was prescient when he wrote:

> You could not see a cloud, because
> No cloud was in the sky:
> No birds were flying overhead –
> There were no birds to fly.

Are voluntary bodies fighting a losing battle? Some seven and a half million birds were traded internationally in 1987, many illegally. Greedy people cruelly exploit man's love for birds. Perhaps a million die in transit. In the European Community alone, despite the Birds Directive, millions are killed, from golden eagles to goldfinches. Passing laws tongue in cheek is easy. Enforcing them is the problem. Without the unremitting pressure of bird-lovers worldwide, governments will continue to shirk their responsibilities through apathy, ignorance or deliberate evasion.

Although firmly rooted on the parliamentary back benches, one may enjoy an occasional success. The curlew and the redshank can thank the Lords for protecting them by insisting on my amendment against the Government's wishes. I hope my obituary (but not yet, please,) will say that, with a few good friends in both Houses, I was one of the birds' MPs.

12
ANIMALS IN WAR
by Jilly Cooper

Jilly Cooper, the celebrated author and journalist, has a deep concern for animals and has always maintained that their services to mankind have not been adequately recognised. In 1983 she wrote a book, Animals in War, *recalling the significant role played by animals in man's battles through the ages, from Hannibal's elephants to the horses, mules, dogs and pigeons which have seen active service in modern times.*

We have selected four stories – three of dogs and one of a cat – which demonstrate the bravery of the ordinary domestic pet and its invaluable effect on the morale of the serving soldier.

RATS – THE DOG SOLDIER

Easily the most famous of postwar mascots, Rats, the jaunty little mongrel, adored soldiers and for many years attached himself to different British army units in Crossmaglen, one of the most threatened Northern Ireland trouble spots.

Serving with the Grenadier Guards, the Marines, the Queen's Own Highlanders and the Welsh Guards, Rats went on ceaseless patrols, car chases and helicopter flights, when he gave everyone heart attacks, leaping thirty feet to the ground, as the helicopter came down to land.

He was shot at more times than anyone could remember; he was blown up by bombs, including a firebomb which burnt several inches off his tail. Four pieces of metal lay trapped along his spine; shotgun pellets still lodged in his chest; he was run over twice by cars in the course of duties, leaving him with permanently bent paws. Worst of all, being such an affectionate dog, he had to suffer the heartbreak of losing a beloved master and finding a new one each time a unit moved on.

Gradually his fame spread, and he became not only an IRA hit target, but also a national celebrity, receiving two sacks of mail a day, which took six fulltime soldiers to answer. He was also given numerous presents from admirers, including one old lady who sent him last week's copy of the *Radio Times* and *TV Times* each week.

His greatest service to the army, however, was boosting morale. 'At the head of the patrol, half strutting, half waddling briskly and happily ahead, he gave the illusion that all was right with the world and death and violence merely a bad dream.'

Or as another soldier who served with him said, 'Rats was an oasis of friendship in a desert of sadness.'

Finally in 1980 the exertions of war took their toll on his small frame. On doctor's orders, he was given an honourable retirement, and a very distinguished passing-out parade. Now he lives happily in Kent, where new hobbies include chasing the local pheasants.

BOBBY OF MAIWAND

Bobby, a white mongrel, was attached to the 2nd Battalion, the Royal Berkshire Regiment, with whom he went to India when the Afghan War broke out. He was present at the famous Battle of Maiwand in 1880 when the British were overwhelmed by an enemy ten times their number. His battalion was gradually whittled down, until they were all killed and only Bobby, who'd stood barking defiantly at the head of the gallant little band throughout the engagement, was left. Taken prisoner, he later joined the remnants of the regiment, at Kandahar. Back in England, Bobby, wearing a smart scarlet coat trimmed with fake pearls, was presented to Queen Victoria. She listened to his story with rapt attention, begged to see his back where he'd been wounded, and pinned the Afghan Medal on his collar. After being taken up by royalty, Bobby became very much above himself, and refused to fraternise with any of the local dogs. Nemesis descended in the form of a hansom cab which ran him over in Gosport. Queen Victoria is said to have cried when she heard this sad news.

PRINCE – THE MIRACLE FINDER

Prince, an Irish terrier, was devoted to his master, Private James Brown of the North Staffordshire Regiment, and was quite inconsolable when Mr Brown was posted to France in September 1914. Then one day he disappeared from his home in Hammersmith, and to everyone's amazement turned up at Armentières a few weeks later, and tracked down his master in the trenches in a frenzy of delight. Because no one could believe the story, the Commanding Officer had master and dog paraded in front of him next morning. Evidently Prince had cunningly attached himself to some troops who were crossing the Channel, and by some sixth sense had managed to locate his master. He became the hero of the regiment, and fought beside his master for the rest of the war.

SIMON – THE CHAMPION RATTER

Simon, a handsome black and white cat, belonged to the captain of HMS *Amethyst*, and was given to strolling across the knees of his master's guests at dinner, and sitting on the chart whenever a course was being laid. On 20 April 1949 Simon was thrust into war, when Chinese Communist batteries opened fire on his ship in the Yangtze river. A shell landed on the captain's cabin, killing his master, wounding Simon in several places, and singeing his fur and whiskers. For a few days he took refuge, but the shelling had shaken numerous rats out of their normal hiding place. Simon therefore left the comfort of the captain's cabin, and lodged in the Petty Officer's mess to be nearer the scene of operations and to make his raid on the rats. His catches were so numerous that they were recorded on a list. When the ship escaped on 31 July, Simon carried on ratting. News of his heroism preceded him, and when the crippled *Amethyst* limped into Hong Kong, numerous letters, telegrams, tins of food, and cheques to buy cream awaited him. Sadly, in quarantine he missed his ship mates so much, he pined away and died, but was later awarded a 'Pussthumous' Dickin Medal.

13
A SUCCESSION OF CATS
An interview with David Davis MBE MA (*Oxon*)

*David Davis retired in 1970 after a distinguished career in the
BBC. For many years he was Head of 'Children's Hour' and his
voice became universally well loved through his readings and
recordings of children's stories. An accomplished musician (LRAM,
ARCM) he was originally taken on as an accompanist for 'Children's Hour' and he has composed and published a number of
songs and put together an anthology of children's poems and prose
for Christmas:* A Single Star.

*An animal lover, David Davis has always had a cat in the
house, and here he talks of his pets and their place in his family
life.*

When my wife and I married, we had a Scottie bitch of which
we were very fond. After she was horribly run over and killed,
we could not face having to choose another dog. Instead we
had a cat, and for the remainder of our very happy married
life there was a succession of cats in the house – five altogether,
mostly one at a time. I can remember the names of them all:
Tibby, Tarquin, Quince, Spike and Guy. The last two, Spike
and Guy, both left their autographs on their favourite chair
and, since my wife died in 1982 and Guy departed the same
year, I have not had the heart to have it re-upholstered.

They were all affectionate cats. Some cats are so aloof that
you cannot get very close to them, but they all command
respect. You must not expect them to do as you ask; they will
always please themselves and do as they wish. They are so
different, in that respect, from dogs, who always want to
please their master. Nevertheless, they have a special quality

of peace and when they are sitting on your lap, in front of the fire, being stroked and gently purring, there is nothing more relaxing.

Each of our cats had a distinct personality and they all had their own charming little habits. One used to come and put his paws on the table, when we were at our meal, asking for attention. Another would sit for hours at a time in the espalier tree in the garden, in a sort of Buddha-like attitude, completely still. Cats are very enigmatic; they give the impression that their thoughts are elsewhere.

Our first cat was still with us at the outbreak of war and accompanied us in the evacuations and moves. First we moved with the BBC down to Bristol. I remember the cat's behaviour during the awful night raid in 1940. While we were cowering in the cellar, that little creature Tibby just went out into the garden and sat, looking up into the sky, completely unmoved by the bombs dropping around the area.

We have a cottage in Wales, and after the war we used, of course, to take our cat with us, together with the children. That road journey, when I go to the cottage nowadays, is indelibly marked for me by the memory of dramatic incidents – the place where a child or the cat was sick, or where we ran into one of the inevitable crises visited upon families in transit.

Our second cat, Tarquin, is not such a happy memory. He ran away and was never seen again. It is heartrending when a cat disappears and one can only wonder what has happened to him. All the roads in my neighbourhood of London are plastered with pathetic notices seeking information about lost cats and kittens, and very often, I am sure, the animal has been the centre of a single person's life. It is like losing a close friend without explanation.

One often hears stories of cats disappearing and returning to the former home when a family moves house – missing for weeks and then turning up bedraggled and starving at the old address. Fortunately that never happened to us. The area where I live is now filling up with cats. Two new families have recently moved in nearby, with three cats between them. They wander round the gardens, which has had a sad effect on the bird population. The cats have not caught any, but they have driven all the birds away.

Earlier on in the summer I used to have tea in the garden; the birds would come and we would have tea together. There was a family of six sparrows, and two blackbirds, and they were fascinating – especially the sparrows. One of the family was either blind or mentally handicapped, and all through the summer it just stood there while the other sparrows came and fed it. At the beginning I assumed it was a fledgling, but by the end of the summer I felt there had to be another explanation.

Up at the cottage in Wales I used to have a bird bath for the little ones and we were able to observe a lovely collection of chaffinches, blue tits and great tits, but on my last visit I found the garden had been taken over by a pair of magpies. Beautiful as these birds are, they frighten away all the smaller birds and our little families had disappeared. They are also very greedy. As soon as you put out bread or crumbs, they swoop down and prevent any other birds sharing in the food.

Since my wife died I have travelled frequently, and when our last cat, Guy, died the same year, I decided it would be unfair to have another one who would have to spend three or four weeks at a time in a cattery. So I am left with memories of a whole line of feline companions, stretching over many years, and I shall never forget the exodus of Guy, the last one. He developed a large growth and he had to be put down. I took him to the vet and asked if I might hold him while the injection was being prepared. Guy sat with absolute calm until, after the injection, his little legs quietly folded and he went down. It was a death of total dignity.

14
THE HIDDEN BENEFACTORS
by Gerald Durrell OBE

Gerald Durrell needs no introduction to animal lovers. His many books, all based on his vast personal experience, are universally read and treasured. His zoo in Jersey gives interest and pleasure to visitors from all over the world and his television programmes have made a significant contribution to our knowledge and appreciation of wildlife. We asked him for a basic comment on the place of animals in our world and he has invited us to quote the following extract from his book The Stationary Ark.

It is obvious that the human race is still woefully ignorant of how the world works. In many parts of the planet, we are destroying with such ferocious rapidity that there is not even time to give a name to or scientifically to describe what we are destroying, let alone to discover its importance, biologically speaking. It is as well to remember that, when we exterminate a species, we endanger or destroy with it a host of satellite creatures that depend upon it for their existence. When you chop down a tree, you are not just killing a tree, you are destroying the equivalent of a vast and teeming city, because there are so many different forms of creature that live upon it. What we are doing can have far-reaching effects; effects which may not be apparent on the surface; effects which ultimately may rebound upon mankind in an unpleasant way. People comfort themselves with the old saying: 'You can drive nature out with a pitchfork, but she will return'. The word to note here is 'pitchfork'. When pitchforks were the most up-to-date weapon in man's armoury against nature, this was, of course, true; but now you are driving nature out with pesticides, bulldozers, chain-saws, man-made floods and man-made filth – relentlessly, thoroughly and speedily, so she cannot return.

I get very tired of people asking me what *use* are the animals I am trying to preserve? What use can some obscure tropical creature be to a man in Sydney, or Chicago, or Stalingrad, or Peking?

The answer comes in two parts. First, we have no shred of moral right to exterminate a species which has taken millions of years to evolve and which has as much right on this planet as we have. In fact, it has now more right to be here, since it has not tried to step outside its allotted place in nature and is, in most cases, of benefit to its environment in consequence. This cannot be said of so-called civilised mankind, however sanguine your view of your own species. Second, if one must adopt the arrogant and God-like attitude that a thing should only exist if it is of use to man (that chapter in Genesis has a lot to answer for), then the reply to 'what use are they?' is simply that, as yet, we have not the remotest idea of what is and what is not of benefit to mankind.

There are thousands of examples which show clearly how, first of all, we have to know how the world functions, before we can manipulate it to our benefit, without destroying it; and how the most obscure and unlikely creature may turn out to be of enormous use to us. Let us take just three.

In England, the county of Sussex was famous for its white clover and, indeed, large numbers of people depended upon this crop for their livelihood. Then the clover suddenly and mysteriously started to fail and whatever the farmers did was of no avail. In desperation, as a last resort, they turned to a biologist for help – something they should have done in the first place. That they happened to choose a man called Charles Darwin was fortuitous. Having investigated the problem, Darwin informed the worried farmers that what they wanted was more cats; a remark which led the stalwart sons of the soil to believe that the old boy must have taken leave of his senses.

It appeared that there was only one sort of Bumble bee

which had a proboscis long enough to fertilise the rather complex clover flower. This bee built its nests in the banks in the hedgerows. A species of fieldmouse lived in the banks; a rodent with a sweet tooth, who would dig out the bees' nests and eat the honey and the young. It appeared that the fieldmice were having a population explosion and the number of natural predators had not risen sufficiently fast to cope with this. The rodents' depredations on the bees' nests were becoming so great that the results were showing in the poor clover crops.

In Brazil, they decided that it was silly to have such an important crop as the Brazil nut scattered about the forest in the untidy way that nature had arranged. It was obviously more sensible to grow them in rows in plantations, like any other crop. This was done, and the trees grew, prospered and flowered, but to the mystification of all they produced no nuts. Belated investigation disclosed a situation somewhat like the Bumble bees and the clover. Apparently the flower of the Brazil nut tree has been adapted so that it can only be pollenised by one species of bee, which has strength enough to raise a kind of trap-door to get into the flower. Now this insect found that on a plantation it had no nectar to feed on when the Brazil nut tree was not in flower, so, not surprisingly, it ignored the unnatural plantations and remained in the forest, where it had a sufficient supply of food all the year round.

Then there is the case of the humble armadillo – a sufficiently obscure animal, you would have thought, to have been useless to a human being anywhere, except possibly for food, or (in the case of the Paraguayans) for making guitars out of their skins. However, it seems possible that this inoffensive creature may prove to be of enormous use to mankind. Experiments suggest that the armadillo could help in the eradication of leprosy. This creature, perhaps because it has an extraordinarily low body temperature, is the only one in which the human *Lepra* bacillus proliferates in sufficient amounts to be potentially useful in the creation of a vaccine against leprosy. Furthermore, it is believed by cancer researchers that the study of leprosy patients will provide them with the knowledge as to why people suffering from cancer fail to reject their tumours.

It should be clear from these three examples, that what we are basically in need of most urgently is knowledge of how our world functions.

15
THE GIANT PANDA
by HRH The Duke of Edinburgh

His Royal Highness Prince Philip, Duke of Edinburgh, spoke of the plight of the giant panda in his keynote speech to the World Wildlife Fund/Asahi Forum in Tokyo in 1984. The Prince has kindly invited us to quote the following extract from the speech, as published in his book Down to Earth.

The situation of the giant panda in western China illustrates virtually all the problems confronting the world of living nature. Unfortunately I have to say that all these problems derive from one basic source – the phenomenal success of one particular species – *Homo sapiens*.

For generations human communities existed in a general balance with the natural world. Occasionally it happened that one civilisation or another became particularly successful and expanded much faster than others. In ancient times this happened to the Mayans in Central America, to the Hittites in Asia Minor, to the people of Mesopotamia and of the Indus Valley. In every case they consumed the raw materials, provided by their natural resources, faster than those resources could regenerate and the civilisation collapsed. As a consequence most of those areas became deserts and have remained so ever since.

In modern times the differences are, firstly that the basic materials for industrial communities are minerals and other non-renewable resources, and secondly that the scientific and industrial revolutions have made it possible for the world's population to increase beyond anything known in history. It is now four times what it was 200 years ago and there is every chance that it will increase from over 4,000 million today to 6,000 million by the end of the century. This time when the resources run out the whole human complex is likely to collapse.

There is one very simple rule; it is that the planet earth can only sustain a certain volume of life. We live on a globe that cannot expand so that the more people inhabiting the earth, the less room there is for any other form of life. Just look around Tokyo. Apart from the human population how much other life manages to exist?

Look at China – the population today is about 1,000 million, roughly equivalent to the population of the whole world 200 years ago. As was absolutely inevitable, this huge increase has resulted in the demand for more food from more agricultural land; more natural resources, such as timber and fish; more pollution from human and industrial effluent; more soil erosion, and the consequent reduction in the space available for the populations of wild animals and plants.

The giant pandas used to roam in bamboo forests that stretched throughout the whole of western China and covered millions of square kilometres. Today, human encroachment and exploitation have reduced the forests to about 30,000 square kilometres. It is only due to their rarity and shyness that pandas have not suffered quite so seriously as other animals as a result of the commercial demand for their skins or as food. Not quite so seriously, but quite seriously enough.

Without taking moral and ethical requirements or emotional attitudes into consideration, there is no purely 'conservation' reason for prohibiting the exploitation of wild species for commercial or sporting purposes, provided such exploitation is limited by the ability of species to produce a sustainable surplus.

Conservation means the survival of species, and to achieve the conservation of species we need the help, support and involvement of all nations. It is the responsibility of the richer nations – such as Japan – to help the less wealthy nations to conserve their natural heritage.

Pandas also inevitably suffer from the other consequences

of human encroachment; particularly disturbance, erosion and pollution. Pandas may be fortunate for the time being in that their bamboo forests are only affected by encroachment and the natural cycle of die-back and re-growth. The future is even bleaker for forest animals in other parts of the world which are affected by the more insidious menace of acid rain.

It may be comforting to imagine that it is only necessary to control the human influence on the survival of pandas, but the degradation of the environment cannot be put into reverse quite so easily. In fact many of the effects of human interference can never be reversed. In any case extinction is forever.

Similarly, it may seem that all is not lost while it is possible to breed pandas in captivity. All may not be lost, but is there really much point in maintaining a captive population if there is no prospect whatever of reintroducing them to their natural habitat because in the meanwhile it has simply disappeared?

The panda illustrates the real dilemma and the serious challenge to mankind. The fact is that this dilemma has to be resolved in our generation. If we in this generation do nothing to give the rest of the living world a chance to survive, we will be signing its death warrant. For those who prefer to be more concerned with human welfare and human survival, let me just say that the death of nature also means the death of mankind.

16
WHOSE WORLD IS IT?
An interview with Barry Fantoni

Novelist, broadcaster, cartoonist and jazz musician, Barry Fantoni has been a member of the editorial staff of Private Eye *for twenty-five years and the 'Diary' cartoonist of* The Times *since 1983. He also designs posters and book jackets and has held many one-man exhibitions. His musical compositions are well known in the jazz world and his books include* Barry Fantoni's Chinese Horoscope *(1985). He holds committed views on the place of animals in society and here he outlines his philosophy.*

I often hear it said that respect between human beings will lead to respect for animals, but I believe the truth to be the other way round. Human respect has to be developed over a period. It is not something given to you at birth; you have to spend your growing years earning and acquiring it. Dignity is the same. Animals, on the other hand, have a natural inborn dignity and an attitude towards other creatures, including man, which is void of malice and, at the same time, full of trust.

I was a war baby, born in the East End of London in 1940, and apart from a few stray cats there were no animals around, except horses, and I can still vividly recall the sound of their hooves in the street. When the air raids began, we had our house redesigned by the Luftwaffe with a see-through ceiling and I was sent to the country. That was my first real introduction to animals other than domestic pets and it opened up a new world for me.

Returning home after the war, I began to develop an antipathy towards eating animals. Coming from an Italian-Jewish background, I found myself forced into eating them all the time. The weekends I dreaded. A typical Jewish Saturday for us meant pickled fish, crab, huge plates of beef – and then, with the Italians on Sunday there would be salami, spaghetti bolognese and veal escalope. My five-year-old stomach could not cope with the intake of meat and fish, and I recall that period of my childhood being dogged almost incessantly by stomach complaints. My mother's remedy – lying on my back with a hot-water bottle – turned me into a pitiful physical weed.

Enlightenment came when, at the age of thirteen, I was sent to the Camberwell School of Art. There I met people from different cultures, and among the teachers were two vegans, one of whom had a leaning towards the East and made me think about the way I should eat and my attitude to animal life. When I left home at sixteen, I took summer work in a bakery at Brixton, where I met a Hungarian vegetarian. Through his friendship and influence I too became a dedicated vegetarian.

Once we make a decision not to eat animals, it conditions our thinking about the place of animals in society and in the world. This is a very important step, as ninety per cent of man's cruelty to animals is as a result of preparing them for slaughter, and often the slaughter itself.

As children we learn respect for animals, but before long we seek to destroy that respect. We discover that we can treat animals as we please, irrespective of their sufferings, and it is only one stage further to assume that people can be similarly treated.

I tend to opt out of religious systems, most of which are based on the principle of a supreme head and a hierarchy of lesser creatures, ending up with the ant which can be crushed underfoot. I see man and animal running in parallel lines and I hope to respond to the needs of animals in an instinctive way. If I see a dog running in the street and looking lost or distressed, I will stop and do something about it.

On the plane returning from Seattle recently, one hour from arrival at Heathrow, people in front of us started climbing on to the seats and screaming. I thought the plane must be about to crash, but it transpired that a hamster had been seen running around, and because the plane was full of Americans, they were all hysterical. They probably imagined it was some kind of extraterrestrial being and they were completely incapable of dealing with it. Even the stewardesses were absolutely useless. By chance we were sitting at the rear of the cabin, our request for seats in the non-smoking section having produced the opposite result, and for most of the flight I was feeling physically sick. However, the poor little hamster eventually ended up nearby and disappeared into the cubicle where the cabin staff kept their equipment. I managed to get hold of the frightened creature and put it in the top pocket of my jacket. I asked for an empty cardboard box and made some airholes in it, lined it with paper and tissues, and put a piece of cake in it. It made a happy and safe home for the hamster until we reached Heathrow. At one stage, when I looked into the box, I thought it was dead. It was lying on its back, feet in the air, but on further inspection I realised he was fast asleep! When we arrived – by this time he was named Panam – I took responsibility for him and paid his quarantine fee. He now resides in a zoo in Norwich, and that episode sums up my attitude towards an instinctive response to animals.

We have two cats and two dogs at home. Archie and Jelly Roll Morton are blue roan cocker spaniels. I discovered dogs through my wife, and since knowing them I have realised how much there is to be learnt, both about animal care and about our own behaviour. Cockers like human companionship, they like to be near you and to be part of your life. It has been said that a dog has a brain equivalent to a child of five, and if you accept that, it is a guide to your treatment of them.

Human beings have the ability to be dignified and to act in a dignified way to fellow creatures. It is degrading to assume a dominant position and to treat them as possessions. Our relationship with animals is the first step to understanding the harmony of nature, and I believe we severely damage our own status if we fail to respect their place in society.

17
MARMOSETS AND TAMARINS
by Lady Rosamund Fisher

Fifteen years ago Lord and Lady Fisher of Kilverstone turned their Norfolk estate into a wildlife park and formed the Kilverstone Wildlife Charitable Trust. Principally intended for the preservation and protection of animals of Latin-American origin, giant anteaters, armadillos, llamas and Falabella miniature horses from Argentina figure among the more unusual residents, but we have asked Lady Rosamund Fisher to tell us something about her experiences with two delightful species of South American monkeys – the marmoset and the tamarin.

These small monkeys are among the only monkeys in the world that normally give birth to twins, not to single babies. Quite often triplets may be born. When this happens, one baby may die or may be rejected. Biologically it makes much more sense for the species to rear two healthy young that live, rather than trying to rear three weak babies that may all die due to insufficient milk. At Kilverstone, if triplets are born, we remove one baby, which I rear by hand, leaving the parents with the twins with which they are able to cope.

Marmosets and tamarins have 'women's lib' worked out to a fine art! Father does all the work of carrying the babies around, only handing them over to mother at feeding time. After feeding, mother hands them straight back to him. In the wild the responsibility of carrying the young is a heavy one – in more than one sense. It is from this position that the young learn what is safe or dangerous, what is good to eat and what is poisonous. As the family grows – and the norm is for them to give birth twice a year – the elder twins help father in carrying and caring for the younger siblings, thus learning to be good parents in the future. They are taking a weight off dad's shoulders – literally.

Marmosets and tamarins bring up their families firmly and with strict rules and regulations. Many young human parents could take a leaf from their book! One of the prime rules appears to be that the youngest and weakest of the group is cared for first and foremost. The babies go up to the parents and older siblings and take the food from their mouths, and it is always given to them. In this way the young wean themselves – by observing their elders and following suit.

Once, I was watching one of our large groups of red-mantled tamarins while they were feeding. One of the baby twins approached an older sibling – a teenager in our terms – and demanded the food he was eating. This happened to be a grape, the most favoured of all food, and the teenager saw no reason to part with the tasty morsel to his baby sister. So he carried on eating and ignored the begging youngster. Father, who was only a little chap a mere seven inches long, saw this scenario, dashed across the cage and boxed the teenager's ears while yelling abuse at him, whereupon the youngster delved into his mouth and fished out a miniscule piece of grape, which he handed to his little sister. I am sure he didn't forget his lesson from father.

We had a Cotton Eared Marmoset who gave birth to triplets. We left the three babies with the parents for a few hours, as usual, in the hope that all three would suckle and thus get a little colostrum or 'first milk' which contains antibodies from the mother that will give the young some immunity against infection. The keeper must keep a close watch on the parents knowing that they might cast one baby off since they are only able to rear two. When a baby has to be removed or is rejected, I go into my now familiar routine – boiling kettles, filling a baby's hot water bottle, mixing and heating up SMA human baby milk to fill the tiny bottle I use, and plugging in the incubator to heat up.

This particular little Cotton Eared Marmoset was a boy, called Dandelion because as he grew he developed that lovely fluffy look of the Dandelion seed-head. When Dandy, as he was soon called for short, was two weeks old, I was brought his two siblings, as the mother was ill with 'Marmoset wasting disease'. One of the two sisters, Lego, had a broken leg and had to be taken to the vet to have her leg set in plaster which resembled a string vest or net when wet, but quickly set hard. The last triplet was tiny, only half the size of the other two so she was called Weency which turned into Wincey Willis in no time.

So I reared Dandy, Lego and Wincey Willis, starting on SMA, then progressing to Milupa, a human baby weaning food. Later a little mashed banana is introduced and thence onto a 'fruit salad'. Twins are bad enough to feed – each fighting for the one bottle, but triplets are definitely worse!

Dandy always remained very tame and humanised – he would always leave his sisters to jump onto my shoulder and would have happily ridden around there all day if I had let him. Great though the temptation is to have a wild animal who loves you more than he loves his own kind, it's not right. It is important for the animals in captivity to live normal lives in groups of their own kind and not to be too humanised, but at the same time they have to learn to cope with the presence of humans in close proximity. Monkeys particularly adapt very quickly to the human presence, and notably recognise and greet members of staff and are curious and interested in the public. It is equally important, however, that the monkeys are able to recognise their own kind as mates and to be able to fit into the complexities of the primate social structure.

This was why we were so depressed about having to hand rear these triplet marmosets. It is well known that marmosets and tamarins when hand-reared, do not observe and help in the rearing process as described above, and will most often kill, mutilate or reject their babies when they themselves give birth. We had first hand experience of this when we acquired some Cotton Topped Tamarins from a laboratory. We were so pleased to be able to give these animals roomy inside quarters and a spacious garden of their own after the cramped steel cages in which they had been confined. Laboratories are not concerned with breeding and maintaining the population gene pool of endangered species as zoos are, so when these highly endangered Cotton Tops bred, the offspring were separated from the parents upon weaning and became further test specimens. The Cotton Tops that we rescued killed their babies, because they had never learned how to care for them.

So here I was hand-rearing triplet marmosets – I couldn't let them die but what was the future for them? When they were about a year old, we received Smuggles B-Cal – so called because he was smuggled into this country on a British Caledonian flight from Brazil in an Italian's pocket. He was only tiny, but even very young marmosets have a piercing, high pitched squeal, which the air hostess obviously noticed. On landing at Gatwick, customs were informed and Smuggles was confiscated. We were contacted and asked if we would have him. I felt very sorry for the little chap, since he had to undergo six months in our Quarantine house and do without much in the way of cossetting and play.

When six months was up, we put him in with Lego and they got on well together – so well that Lego soon showed a thickening waistline. 'Oh dear' I thought, 'more problem children that will need to be hand-reared.' Time went by and Lego produced only a single baby, so I went to see her and was expecting to have to take the baby away. To my amazement Lego was being a perfect mother, both feeding and carrying her baby. We named the baby 'Lego's child' as a tribute to her, since Smuggles was no help at all, but at least he didn't attack the baby as sometimes happens. Lego continued to care for the youngster alone, but when the baby was about eight weeks old, Smuggles did start to play with it, although he only seemed to want an occasional romp around. Six months later Lego gave birth to twins and this time Smuggles took on the full responsibilities of fatherhood, with Lego's child in attendance. Now they are a large family group, all behaving in a normal way – and we are very proud of them.

18
THE TALE OF TWO DASSIES
by Susan Fowkes

We have received this delightful story from Mrs Fowkes, who, with her husband Steven, runs a wildlife sanctuary in South Africa known as World of Birds. The dassie, or rock rabbit, is only found in South Africa, but after reading Susan Fowkes' description, this is undoubtedly the rest of the world's loss.

Breeding season is a wonderful time. Especially when I end up being Mum to lots of little orphans. The worst of it is that there is no such thing as an early night. The best part is the fun.

At the end of October we received two terrific little rock rabbits, about the size of a rat with no tail. They had fat cheeks and black button noses, and they had what I called 'tupperware teeth' – two flat, plastic-looking, white rounded teeth at the top, and a row of tiny teeth on the bottom, short in the centre and longer on the outer edge. They had pale eyebrows, and their mouths were outlined with the same colour, giving the impression of a permanent silly grin. Their hair was thick and brown, fairly coarse on top and soft on the belly. In between the brown were black hairs, sensitive to the touch, which would grow stiff and thick up to six or seven centimetres long when adult, acting as guard hairs to inform the animal how close it was to any object. If I touched the tips of these hairs with the palm of my hand, the animals would whirl round, pretending to be vicious and threatening to bite. It was a game which, like most baby animal behaviour, was practice for more serious things to come during adult life.

The books say that for ninety-five percent of the time,

dassies in the wild are extremely busy doing practically nothing. Mine weren't like that at all. Like most kids, they thought that good, healthy food was boring. They preferred to chew leisurely on more interesting items, favourites being elastic, plastic, cotton wool and plastic-coated wire.

Right from the start, he was aggressive with the bottle, trying to break the teat off to chew, and she was always a problem to feed. When they had settled down after a few days, I could call them with a *tut-tut-tut* sound and both would come running, more often than not bringing whatever they were busy with, such as an earbud or a cigarette (they enjoyed the filters) dangling from one side of their mouths.

We went through a series of names – first Hansel and Gretel, which didn't really stick. Then Chew and Chomp seemed very apt. When he started practising to be a boy, it was Romeo and Juliet, and finally, because nothing really fitted, He and She.

Their greatest game was to jump on top of our kitchen dustbin, which is the flip-top type. When they fell in they would squeal until Mum came to rescue them, only to jump up again the second they were on the ground. They certainly kept me running.

Certain things about them made them completely different from just about any other animal, except perhaps the elephant, who is their closest relative. On the front feet they have nice round toes, with little flat toenails like yours and mine. The back feet have three toes, two with toenails and one with a claw like a dog's. They use this claw for scratching and grooming, and it is such a pleasure to have an animal baby that sits on one's shoulder but doesn't dig in its claws to hang on. Unfortunately, they don't have a 'handle', such as a tail, so if they slip they have to jump. They have nictitating membranes – a third eyelid which enables them to gaze directly into the sun – and they are the only animal that has two appendixes.

If I lay on my stomach on the floor, they would come running for a cuddle, and it became a routine. She would jump on to the back of my neck and curl round to suck one of her back claws, accompanied by a strange guttural grunting which immediately triggered a hunger reaction in him. He would first sniff my left ear to make sure it was the one he wanted, and then suck my earring, with a constant soft but high-pitched squeal, which was quite loud when directed into one's ear! When he was a little older, he would start off with my ear, then gaze into space with his tongue out, sucking thoughtfully.

Unlike bushbabies and monkeys, dassies don't urinate on their hands and feet to ensure a grip. The pads on their feet actually sweat, and dassies are able to climb up and down almost vertical surfaces. They are unable to retain body temperature effectively and die quite easily from heat or cold. At night they huddle together for warmth, but in a circle facing outwards, probably to avoid the arguments they tend to have when face to face with each other. They love to sunbathe, lying on their sides or on their bellies with all legs stretched out, absorbing every bit of warmth from the rocks underneath and the sun above. No less than twenty-one different vocalisations have been recorded, including grunts, growls, wails, squeals, twitters, snorts, whistles and chirrups.

It was Christmas time and the usual decorations adorned the house. All Christmas presents were wrapped in paper specially decorated and signed by little dassie teeth. The tree had to be climbed, tasted and enjoyed, and She especially loved chocolate. If it was wrapped in silver foil, then so much the better. We had little chocolate bells and baubles hanging on the tree, and of course each one was sampled. He, however, preferred balloons. The ones hanging on the wall could be reached by standing on the back of the rocking chair and stretching very hard. If lucky enough to find one on the floor, he would sit and contemplatively chew on the knot. When, as would invariably happen, the balloon popped, he wouldn't even flinch. He would hesitate for three seconds or so, and continue chewing. Many a time did I rush to rescue a long piece of elastic or other such chewing stuff, to prevent it from disappearing down the throat and into what had to be a cast-iron stomach.

On one occasion my husband Steven and I were cleaning

the swimming pool at my parents' house as they were away for Christmas. The dassies, of course, were with us. They had a free run of the fenced-in area, and were still too young to want to venture far from Mum. He suddenly decided that he wanted to be on the other side of the pool, but didn't notice the large expanse of water between 'here' and 'there'. In mid-run, he found himself in deep water. Without hesitation, Steven dropped everything except his clothes and dived to the rescue, shoes and all! He said that from underneath he could clearly see four little feet paddling strongly, and probably needing no help at all except to be lifted out on the other side. So, dassies can swim.

Then She fell ill. She had an upset tummy and none of the usual cures had any effect. On the third visit to the vet it was decided that her insides didn't feel normal, and the likely possibility that she could have eaten something harmful was to be investigated. Before the operation, I stayed up with her all night, trying to encourage her to eat something, because she hadn't had anything during the day. The only food she would eat was a little fish, which she'd never eaten before. All she would drink was some Chamberlain's Colic and Diarrhoea Remedy, and the two of them actually argued over it. I hoped it would give her some sort of relief, because her tummy was so sore that she whistled faintly all the time and didn't know whether to sit, stand or lie on the heating pad. She seemed to gain a little strength by morning, but not enough. She survived the operation, but didn't regain consciousness. Perhaps she wasn't well from the beginning, but it was a tragic loss which affected us all very badly, especially her little brother. He went into mourning, and nothing I could do would shake him out of his depression. He was very lonely without his playmate and I gave him a small teddy bear to snuggle up to at night. After the second night he started to become a little more independent, and on the third day he suddenly snapped out of it and I became his best friend. He went everywhere with me and began to develop a personality of his own. He loved to jump on the bed in the morning to drink the remains of last night's coffee or tea from the bottom of the mugs, preferring Steven's to mine as it was sweeter. The vet warned me about this. 'Be careful,' he said, 'It's bad for his teeth.' The dassie also tried to get into the sugar bowl, sticking his nose into the hole in the lid for the spoon. Another thing I was warned about was dassies' tendency towards alcoholism, particularly white spirits like cane and vodka. I had noticed that He was quick to jump on my lap to try and share my nightcap of vodka and lemonade. He would put himself to bed in his little house when he was tired, snuggling under the pillowcase which covered his electric blanket, with just the tip of his nose showing.

He loved grapes, milk, Cerelac, banana-flavoured Pro Nutro and pumpkin pips, and I would usually have to try each one until I found out what he was asking for. He would stand upright on his back feet, squealing, telling me in no uncertain terms what he wanted, and wasn't I listening? Oh, and I had to hide packets of biscuits well out of reach. He also enjoyed popcorn. Unfortunately, however, he was convinced that polystyrene was simply stale popcorn, and I certainly needed about thirty hours in the day to keep an eye on him!

The problem of what to call him was still unsolved. For some reason, Steven began calling him Hatsi, and he was soon affectionately known as Hatsi-Bear. And then, two days after our return from a fishing trip, Hatsi died. He didn't give us much warning, or enough time to do anything. True to wild animal instinct, he gave the impression of almost perfect health up to half an hour before he died, although he did become a little less active and wouldn't eat. I panicked and called the vet out of bed, but it was too late to find out what we were dealing with. The post mortem showed a probable viral attack which had damaged his heart irreparably within hours. There was nothing we could have done.

So, another precious part of my life slipped away, and I learnt what I'd do without him. It always seems to be the ones that mean the most that are lost. My dassies gave me beautiful memories and I feel so honoured to have had the privilege of their special company, even for so short a time.

19
MY BIRDS
by Christina Foyle

The daughter of William Foyle, founder of the world's best known bookselling organisation, Christina Foyle has devoted her life to the promotion of literature. For over fifty years she has held the famous Foyle's Literary Luncheons, where book lovers have been able to meet and hear great personalities.

Christina Foyle is well known as an animal lover and a friend of birds, who feature largely in her daily life, both at home in Essex and at her London flat above the bookshop.

I love all animals and any, and every, suffering creature finds a home with me. I have twelve cats, six peacocks, four tortoises and a dog, but my particular favourites are the birds and over the years I have made real friends with them.

Years ago my husband and I went to Canada and came back by sea. It was winter and very cold and, as the ship left the St Lawrence River and steamed out to sea, there were great ice floes floating on the water. Every morning there was a very sad sight – scores of little sparrows frozen to death on the deck. One morning we found one that still had a little life in him and we took it to our cabin. We warmed it and fed it and called it Joey. He became our friend on the nine-day journey and used to perch on my shoulder. Joey was different from English sparrows – larger, with a distinct copper colour on his feathers.

The ship docked at Greenock and it was time for Joey to go. We opened the cabin window and away he flew. I have often thought of that little Canadian sparrow among the birds of Scotland.

My home is in Essex. There we have every kind of bird and they all have different characters. I love the birds that herald the spring – the cuckoo, and the swallows that nest in the barn.

Among the summer visitors, almost the most beautiful is the jay, with its lovely band of blue. It is domineering and quickly grabs most of the food. Most charming are the blackbird and the thrush – very nice looking birds and delightful songsters – but most of all I love the cheeky little robin who sits by me every day, and the hosts of sparrows.

Most people look upon sparrows as uninteresting ordinary birds but this is quite untrue. Each sparrow has a very strong personal identity. One of my sparrows is very friendly. He comes within a foot of me to pick up crumbs of bread. I talk to him and he loves it. Another has lost his tail and whenever I go out he is immediately on the scene. One is always accompanied by her baby, who shrilly demands to be fed all the time. Watching this greedy baby with its poor mother makes me glad I have no children. Another has some malformation with its wings and flutters all the time.

While I feed the sparrows the great black crows are calling from the trees, asking me not to forget them. We sprinkle the bread on a huge lawn and watch the crows with their wonderful hopping from piece to piece – just as if they were bouncing.

Among all the birds of Essex there is one that visits only occasionally and it is one of the most beautiful sights in the world – the kingfisher. To see it hovering over the fish pool, with its brilliant blue plumage and marvellous wings, is a truly wonderful experience and compensates for the poor fish it takes for food.

The River Blackwater is at the bottom of our garden and is full of bird life. Graceful swans swim up from Maldon. There are hosts of gulls, terns and peewits and, one winter, we were thrilled when a baby seal appeared.

Even in the heart of London, we are surrounded by birds. We have a flat over Foyles and we look across Manette Street to the garden of St Barnabas Chapel where a blackbird has her nest. She sings all day and sometimes flies over our roof.

We have a balcony in the flat, from where you can see the Houses of Parliament. I put corn on the balcony and scores of pigeons feed on it all day. They make the most beautiful arrangement on the balcony – just like a lovely feather fan.

Birds and animals make life happy, warm and interesting. Every animal will respond to love, so let us always cherish them and thank God that English people love animals.

20
CHIMPS – OUR
CLOSE RELATIVES
by Dr Jane Goodall

Dr Jane Goodall is the world's leading expert on chimpanzees, having spent most of the last thirty years studying them in the forests of Gombe in Tanzania. In recent years, she has become the tireless leader of an international campaign to conserve our now endangered closest relatives, to increase our respect for them and to improve the care and living conditions of those already in captivity, in zoos and laboratories.

One day as I sat near David Greybeard at the bank of a tiny trickle of crystal-clear water, I saw a ripe red palm nut lying on the ground. I picked it up and held it out to him on my open palm. He turned his head away. When I moved my hand closer he looked at it, and then at me, and then he took the fruit, and at the same time held my hand firmly and gently with his own. As I sat motionless he released my hand, looked down at the nut, and dropped it to the ground.

At that moment there was no need of any scientific knowledge to understand his communication of reassurance. The soft pressure of his fingers spoke to me not through my intellect but through a more primitive emotional channel: the barrier of untold centuries which has grown up during the separate evolution of man and chimpanzee was, for those few seconds, broken down.

That incident took place in 1963 when I had been observing the behaviour of free-living chimpanzees at the Gombe National Park in Tanzania for three years. It was an extraordinarily significant moment for me personally, and remains, a quarter of a century later, one of my most vivid memories.

David Greybeard was the first chimpanzee I saw using tools – an incredibly exciting and meaningful observation. I can still remember how I crouched behind a screen of vegetation and watched as he picked a piece of grass and pushed it carefully down one of the passages leading into a termite nest. When he pulled it out, there were several termites clinging on with their jaws. David picked them off with his lips and scrunched them up, then continued fishing. Occasionally he picked a twig and stripped it of leaves so that he could insert it into one of the narrow tunnels. He was modifying an object – making it more suitable for a particular purpose. This was not just tool-*using* but actually a crude form of tool-*making*. Until that time this had been the hallmark of the human species: man the tool-maker. Since that far-off day we have learned that the chimpanzees use more objects for a greater variety of purposes than any creature other than man. These tool-using techniques are passed from one generation to the next through observation, imitation and practice.

Chimpanzees are our closest living relatives. They are more similar to us genetically, physiologically and in the structure of the brain than are any other living creatures. Thus it should not surprise us to learn that chimpanzees show a number of intellectual abilities once thought unique to ourselves. They can, for example, solve simple problems by reasoning. Once, before the chimpanzees trusted me completely, I held out a banana to Mike: he was too nervous to take it from my hand and so, after a few moments he broke off a stick, hit the banana to the ground, then picked it up and ate it. In captivity, chimpanzees have been taught three hundred or more signs of ASL (American Sign Language), each representing a word or a series of words. Once learned, each sign or symbol clearly evokes in the mind of the chimpanzee a mental image or concept of the object it represents. If, for example, the chimpanzee is asked in sign language to fetch an apple, he or she can go and find an apple in the next room. Chimpanzees can recognise themselves in mirrors too, showing they have a concept of 'self'. One young female who was bathed and oiled every evening, spontaneously bathed and oiled her doll.

Some of the most remarkable similarities between chimpanzees and ourselves are seen in the postures and gestures of the nonverbal communication patterns – body language. Like us, chimpanzees embrace and hold hands, kiss and pat one another on the back, both during greeting and in the seeking or giving of reassurance. They swagger and wave their arms to intimidate rivals. They reach out their hands, palm up, to beg.

Chimpanzees, like humans, have a long childhood. Youngsters suckle until they are five or even six years old and remain emotionally dependent on their mother for another three to five years. During this time, close bonds develop between the elder child and his or her young brother or sister. Older offspring, even after they have become relatively independent, continue to spend much time with their families, often throughout life.

Some of the most touching stories from Gombe concern the way family members care about each other. Let me share some of these. The first is about old Madam Bee and her fourteen-year-old daughter Little Bee. Madam Bee became paralysed in one arm during an epidemic of polio (for chimps are susceptible to almost all human diseases). In 1974 there was an unusually long hot dry season. Food was scarce and sometimes it was necessary to travel long distances from one feeding place to another. These journeys exhausted Madam Bee. When she finally arrived she sometimes stretched out on the ground, too tired to climb, while her daughter, with grunts of pleasure, began to feed in the trees above. On three separate occasions Little Bee, after feeding for ten minutes or so, climbed down, her mouth and one hand filled with fruits, went over to her mother, and gave her the food from her hand. Mother and daughter then ate contentedly side by side.

And then there was the time when eight-year-old Pom was leading her family through the forest. Three-year-old Prof was following her, while their mother, Passion, brought up the rear. Suddenly Pom spied a large snake curled up at the side of the trail. With a small cry of alarm, her hair bristling with fear, she shot up a tree. But Prof didn't see the snake – or else he didn't recognise possible danger. He continued towards it until, at the last moment, with every hair on end and a huge grin of fear on her face, Pom rushed down, seized little Prof in her arms and climbed with him to safety.

Over the years ten infants between three and five years old have lost their mothers. Five of the orphans were adopted by their older sisters, one by his brother. Three of these infants became so depressed after losing their mothers that they fell sick and died despite the care they received from their siblings. But the others survived, and the manner in which the self-appointed guardians cared for their young brothers and sisters was touching.

The most heart-warming adoption occurred last year when, during an epidemic of some kind of respiratory illness, my old friend Miff died. She left infant Mel, only just over three years old, all alone in the world. For a couple of weeks he wandered about following first one adult, then another. And then, to our amazement, he was adopted by a twelve-year-old nonrelated male, Spindle. Mel was allowed to ride on Spindle's back during travel, and even to cling on to his belly, especially if it was raining. Spindle shared his food with the infant, and he shared his nest at night. He even risked being attacked himself in order to rescue Mel from potentially dangerous social situations. Without this care, Mel, a sickly infant, almost certainly would not have survived.

I could tell many other tales humorous and sad, violent and tender, about these chimpanzees whose history I have had the privilege of documenting. And all the stories combine to give the same message – that there is continuity of consciousness and mind in the evolutionary process as well as continuity of physical structures. Yet even today, even now that it is increasingly acknowledged in scientific circles that nonhuman animals may be sentient, intelligent beings, there are still hundreds of chimpanzees, in different parts of the world, shut up in tiny, steel-barred, barren cages. If only those responsible for these prisoners could spend some time watching the

Gombe chimpanzees. If only they could observe the tenderness and affection shown by a mother to her young infant, watch the reunion between adults when they embrace, or kiss or hold hands, see how a dominant individual calms and reassures a subordinate with gentle patting. If only they could witness the exuberance of a group of chimpanzees arriving at a tree laden with fruit, and hear their excited calling as they enjoy the feast; and know the sense of contentment and peace that comes at the end of a long day when the chimpanzees have made their springy tree-top sleeping platforms and are settling down for the night. For so often these glimpses into the chimpanzee world generate overwhelming shame for the behaviour of our own species – our arrogant assumption that *our* needs, *our* pleasure, *our* wishes must inevitably come first.

And now, one last story. About a captive chimpanzee this time, Old Man, who was rescued from a lab or circus when he was about eight years old and placed, with three females, on a man-made island in a zoo in Florida. He had been there several years when a young man, Marc Cusano, was employed to care for the chimps. 'Don't go on to the island,' Marc was told. 'Those brutes are vicious. They'll kill you.'

For a while Marc obeyed instructions, and threw the chimps their food from his little boat. But then he began to realise that he could not care for them properly unless he established some kind of rapport with them. So he began going ever closer and closer to the shore of the island when he fed them. One day Old Man reached out and took a banana from Marc's hand. How well I remember when, at Gombe, David Greybeard first took a banana from mine. And, as for me with David, that was the start of a relationship of mutual trust between Marc and Old Man. Some weeks later Marc stepped on to the island, and eventually he could groom and even play with Old Man.

Then came the terrible day when Marc, cleaning up the island, slipped and fell on his face and startled the infant who had been born to one of the females. The infant screamed and his mother leaped to attack Marc, biting into his neck. He felt the blood run down his chest. The other two females at once rushed to support their friend. One bit into Marc's wrist, the other into one leg. He had been attacked before, but never with such single-minded ferocity. He thought it was all up for him.

Suddenly Old Man charged up. Physically he pulled the three females off Marc and hurled them away. And he stayed close by, keeping the highly roused, screaming females at bay, as Marc slowly dragged himself to the boat. 'There is no doubt at all but that Old Man saved my life,' Marc told me later, when he was out of hospital.

This, to me, is a symbolic story. If a chimpanzee, and one who has been abused by humans, can reach across the species barrier to help a human friend in need, then surely we, with our greater capacity for compassion, can reach out to help the chimpanzees, and the other animals, who need us so desperately today. Can't we?

21
BRITISH BUTTERFLIES
An interview with Dulcie Gray CBE

Actress, playwright and authoress, Dulcie Gray made her stage debut in repertory in Aberdeen in 1939, the year in which she married her actor husband Michael Denison. They have appeared together in a great many productions, both in the West End and overseas, and in many films, and collaborated on a book, The Actor and his world, published in 1964.

Although perhaps best known for the husband and wife partnership, Dulcie Gray has featured in numerous other plays and films and on television, most recently as Kate Harvey in 'Howards Way'. She has also found time in a busy career to write twenty novels, a book of short stories, two plays, the definitive book on British butterflies and an adventure book for children. She is a Vice President of the British Butterfly Conservation Society.

I was born in Kuala Lumpur and came to England at a very early age to go to a boarding school at Wallingford in Berkshire. My first recollection of butterflies is in a garden in Sussex. My family had rented a house in Cooden Beach for the holidays and my two cousins were staying with us. They and my brother and sister were older than I, and I was appalled to see them all catching butterflies and putting them in a jam jar to die. I thought how awful it was to kill such beautiful creatures and that started me off on my lifelong interest in butterflies.

Worldwide, the subject is enormous and would need a lifetime of study, so I have always concentrated on British butterflies and that classification alone covers no less than seventy species, including migrants. People frequently ask me where is my personal collection. Of course I have no collection; butterflies are to be observed and studied, not to be killed, and I have never understand the human urge to destroy living creatures.

Britain is not the best country for the butterfly. The climate is unsuitable and birds, wasps, mice and spiders are all predators, but today man is fast becoming the greatest danger through his destruction of the natural environment and industrial pollution. Butterflies are essentially influenced by the sun and most will only fly or lay their eggs in sunshine. For instance, the common blue will shut its wings at the approach of rain and will even stop feeding when clouds appear. Rain, of course, is a major enemy, especially to older butterflies who are not in top condition. Their wings become damaged and they are at the mercy of predators.

It is a popular belief that butterflies only live for one day. This is not true – they live for anything from ten days to twenty – and one or two varieties will live for several months.

One of the more amazing stories of butterflies concerns the Large Blue, Britain's rarest butterfly. The egg is laid in the flower of wild thyme, and the caterpillar, after some weeks of normal living on the plant, drops on to the ground, where it is found and adopted by a myrmica ant. The ant takes the caterpillar down into the depths of the ant hill, where the youngest ant grubs are kept. It spends the winter down there, living on the grubs, until it pupates. When the butterfly finally emerges from the chrysalis, it finds its way in the dark along the galleries and out of the ant hill where it has spent ten months. It then climbs up the stem of a plant, and when its wings have dried, it can fly away. It seems sad that after all those months of preparation it mates and dies in about sixteen days.

Many species are rare or endangered, but the common varieties include some of the loveliest, and they can be attracted into one's garden by growing the kind of plants they like to feed on. They are very fond of mauve, and growing mauve buddleia and mauve ice plant will ensure the attendance of butterflies. Similarly lavender, polyanthus, phlox, wallflowers and sweet william are among the plants they favour.

People with gardens could benefit considerably by encouraging the butterflies in this way, especially with the increasing public and government awareness of the importance of conservation. I look forward to a trend away from the traditional neat lawns and tidy flower beds and a change to gardening of a more informal nature, with grass left a little longer on lawns and areas devoted to the growth of wild flowers and plants. Butterflies have been described as the 'mobiles' of the garden and their disappearance would be a great loss. On the other hand, those who choose to foster their preservation by providing for their needs will enjoy untold rewards.

22

AN EQUINE LOVE AFFAIR
An interview with Lucinda Green MBE

One of the country's foremost horsewomen, Lucinda Green has made her name all over the world as a champion three-day event rider. She first captured the public imagination when, at the age of eighteen, she was a member of the winning Junior European Team in 1971. She went on to win many championships at Badminton and Burghley, and represented Great Britain at the Olympic Games in Montreal 1976 and Los Angeles 1984. She has written a number of books about her three-day event horses and her most recent book (1986) is Cross Country Riding.

Lucinda Green's husband David, an Australian three-day eventer, also rides for his country, and they have two children, Freddie, four years old, and baby daughter Lissa.

I was always head over heels in love with horses, like any horse-mad youngster, but in my case I never lost the infatuation. When I approached the age when girls begin to find boys more interesting, I didn't – horses still kept the upper hand.

My parents apparently recognised my unusual affinity with horses, although I myself did not realise it at the time, being a child, but I am told that even a very difficult horse would behave quite normally when I went into its stable. Nevertheless, I was not allowed my own pony until I was nine years old. My mother and father wisely considered that I must learn to ride properly and to look after a pony before owning one, so from the age of four I attended the local riding school.

At fifteen I had my first horse, Be Fair, who in the following seven years took me from the Pony Club to the Olympic

Games, and with him I forged the most exceptional relationship of my life. He was a remarkable horse. He came to me as a bit of a rough rogue, and to begin with he had to go away for a year to various adult riders as I could not make him do anything. When he returned, we started to form a partnership. Looking back, he came to an owner who knew very little, if anything, of actually training a horse, and we had to learn together as we entered the new world of three-day eventing.

Since then I have had other outstanding horses, but Be Fair must always be the special one. He was the first, he put up with my knowing nothing and then, together, we won through to the top.

I believe that to start with such a relationship with a particular horse early in your career is essential in our profession. Then, having reached the top, the difficulty is to stay there, because you will not find that horse again. You have to experiment with new horses, and you soon discover that no two horses are the same, and must be treated as individuals, so the rider is always learning.

Horses may not have the same reasoning powers as humans, but their personalities are equally fascinating, and they must be the most adaptable of all creatures. They will learn the intricate steps of dressage, the art of carriage driving, jumping, racing, steeplechasing – and outside sport they learn the skills of military horses, policing and crowd control and, in many countries, sheep and cattle herding.

Cattle horses in Australia are magnificently trained. I have ridden one, called a cutting-horse champion, and it is an unbelievable experience. You hold on to the pommel of the saddle as he stands stock still, with his forelegs splayed wide, looking from side to side, waiting for the cattle to move. The second they make a move, he shoots to the side and it is all you can do to go the same way and not get thrown in the opposite direction. These horses know exactly what their job is – they have learned to adapt.

To train a horse to Badminton standard will take from four to six years. When you start them at novice level at three feet, they can usually see the other side of the fence – and you proceed together in mutual trust, until you reach Badminton, where you are jumping off the end of the ski jump. All the horse can see is the top branches of the oak trees, but he takes off because he trusts you and because throughout his career you have tried never to break that bond.

The promise of a horse is entirely a matter of heart, and how brave he is. Just as some people are prepared to indulge in dangerous sports or fast driving, while others will not, so is the individual horse. Unfortunately, you do not find out until the big test. For the first time in my life, a little while back, I met one that I do not think had the heart. I spent three years bringing him to the top level, with the one per cent fear in my mind that he might not have the biggest heart in the world, and when we faced his biggest test at Burghley, he literally shook with fright and that was that.

My husband and I are both devoted to three-day eventing but I am not anxious to encourage my children to follow in our footsteps. I think it much better to watch them develop along their own lines. My own parents were fond of horses and keen on riding, but they knew nothing of eventing, so I was able to learn at my own pace and to make my own mistakes, without the frustration of being constantly checked by knowledgeable parents.

I do not admire parents who want nothing more earnestly than for their children to *win* at whatever they do. That, to me, is not the point; it is the partaking and doing your best that matters. The important thing is not the urge to succeed, so much as a desire to enjoy activities and do them well.

23
RIDING FOR CHILDREN
An interview with Harry Greenway MP

Born in 1934, Harry Greenway was educated at Warwick School, the College of St Mark and St John, London, and the University of Caen, Normandy. After a career in teaching, during which he chaired a number of committees on education and the London Schoolboys Hockey Association, he was elected Member of Parliament for Ealing North in 1979.

In 1980 he was awarded the British Horse Society Award of Merit and throughout his years at Westminster he has championed animal causes, in addition to playing a leading part in matters concerning education and the Atlantic Alliance. Harry Greenway is married with one son and two daughters.

I was born on St Francis' Day and, St Francis being the patron saint of animals, my family always sought to teach me to be kind to animals – not that I needed any persuasion.

At the outbreak of World War II, as a very small boy, I had the good fortune to be evacuated from Birmingham to Exmoor, where I lived for the whole of the war years. We used to ride ponies over the moor, sometimes two or three of us on one pony, and I got to know animals of many kinds in their natural habitat, as well as animals in captivity.

My friends and their families were wonderful people and we would go for miles, in any weather, to see other friends. At that time all signposts throughout the country had been removed, to confuse the enemy in the event of an invasion. On occasion, the father of one of my friends, who owned horses, would take us off by car to Taunton, buy ponies and then say 'Ride these back to Minehead!' We boys were only six or seven years of age, but there was very little traffic and we always found our way home. At that age you have no fear, and the ponies knew it too. They never played tricks on us or kicked out if we walked behind them.

After the war I had to leave that splendid setting and go to Warwick School to be educated. I also became a cathedral chorister. Deprived of horses, except for an occasional ride, I began to take notice of domestic pets and I discovered that the closer you get to them the more they reciprocate, and become part of the family. We have recently lost our cat, Batticus. He was a black half-Siamese, eleven years old and such a character. I took him to be put down and it was a heartbreaking experience. There is no question of having a successor yet – it takes time to get over the loss of a friend and member of the family. I must confess I have reservations about some dogs and twice I have been bitten by Alsatians when canvassing at election times. Maybe they didn't like my politics! However, I remain a firm dog-lover all the same.

In 1964, when I was a teacher in London, I founded the London Schools Horse Society, which brought riding and stable management to inner London schoolchildren living in flats where they were not allowed to keep pets. It is most important for children to have the civilising influence which comes through contact with animals, and I founded the organisation for that purpose.

Two years ago the Queen, in conjunction with the Crown Equerry, Sir John Miller, gave me permission to mount a lecture/demonstration in the Royal Mews, called 'The Queen's Horses'. It had never been done before, but Her Majesty graciously permitted it to be held again this year to mark the Silver Jubilee of the Society.

At the height of the Society's activities we had riding and stable-management lessons in one hundred and twenty inner London schools, and the pupils included many disabled children. Parents and grandparents who have come to see me over the years have been grateful for their children's introduction to the horses. In many cases they themselves had been in contact with horses, perhaps as drivers of carriages or milk floats in earlier days, and indeed within living memory there were horse-drawn trams in London. I remember an old man telling me the trams were very hard on the horses. A passenger could stop a tram anywhere, and it was quite usual for the tram to be halted again only a few yards after the horses had started up. A full tram was a very heavy load and it was a great strain on the horses. But his most vivid memory was of the horse manure all over the street, and how people would complain of this terrible pollution which would surely bring the world to an end. Now we regard horse manure as a rare blessing, which of course it is.

During our first twenty-five years, over one hundred thousand children have learned to ride or to handle horses under the scheme, and I calculate that two million more have been influenced through the activities taking place in their schools.

I ride a great deal now. A Member of Parliament has to keep fit and alert, as one works very long hours, and I get up at six o'clock most mornings and ride one of Her Majesty's horses in Rotten Row. This is marvellous exercise, mentally as well as physically, as I have to concentrate and keep my horse fully under control. In my short hour I have to put the horse through a canter and perhaps a gallop, and if I did not have perfect control, I could get into bad trouble when putting the horse into a fast pace.

Since I became a Member of Parliament in 1979, I have worked hard for the cause of animals and I am proud to have been associated with some successes. Two years ago I introduced the Bill which became the Animals Penalties (Amendment) Act 1987. This doubles the penalties for those caught promoting dogfights. We hope the new legislation is holding this disgusting so-called sport at bay, now those caught at it can be sent to prison. People have been known to place bets of as much as fifty thousand pounds on dog fights, with crowds attending, and they are carried out in such secret places, with a clever system of lookouts, that it becomes very difficult for the police to detect. I am glad to say the Act also covers cockfights and similar events.

I also initiated a Bill to disqualify people convicted of cruelty on a first offence from owning animals. Under the previous 1936 Act, anyone disqualified from owning a dog could still own a different animal, but now the ban extends to all animals. I am now, in association with a colleague, sponsoring a Bill to ensure the correct tethering of horses. It has always been legal to tie a cutting rope around the animal's neck and leave it tethered, with no due care. In the future that will be illegal; the owner must provide facilities such as access to water and a swivel chain, and this is a big breakthrough.

Since 1973 I have been an elected member of the British Horse Society Council, and one of our current aims is to clean up horse markets and horse sales. A new code of conduct has been produced by the Farm Animals Welfare Council and I hope we can get a statutory basis to it. It is greatly needed in places like the Southall Horse Market, which has a sorry reputation. It has certainly improved to some extent, but the degree of my success in highlighting the deficiencies of the management is plain. The last time I went there they refused to let me in!

I pray for the day when all mankind understands and properly values the uses of the horse and ceases to abuse it.

24
TWO VEGANS – AND WHY
An interview with Leonard Gregory

An actor for most of his adult life, Leonard Gregory is best known for his portrayal of Detective Sergeant West (Westie) in the popular 'EastEnders'. He is married to Jean Ure, a prolific writer of children's books, and they both deplore the way in which animals are abused in our society. They put the seal on their beliefs when they became vegans, renouncing the personal use of all animal products.

When I was a child I was very frightened of animals. I was a war orphan, brought up in an orphanage, and therefore my exposure to animals at that stage of my life was very limited. There was a system of adoption whereby couples used to come and look at you – rather like a dogs' home, in fact! You were taken out and if, after successive weekends, you fitted in, you were adopted. I was nearly eleven years old when this happened to me and at that time I had many problems to face. I never met either of my parents; my father was unknown and all I know about my mother is that she was finally arrested in Paddington for soliciting.

The social attitudes at that time were based on the theory that the sins of the fathers were visited upon the children, and it was therefore accepted that I would never make a good citizen. It was true that I was very aggressive and antisocial, but I had never had any affection at all in my life. Indeed, the first time my adoptive mother tried to embrace me, before I was adopted, I hit out at her because I did not understand.

Pets of any kind were quite unknown to me and I would scream at the sight of an approaching dog. Then my new parents bought me a puppy for Christmas in the hope of eradicating this aversion. She was a mongrel and she became my constant companion and confidante. My fear disappeared.

When I left school I went to work for a printing house, and for the process of dyeline printing they needed a form of gelatine, one ingredient of which was obtained from the local abattoir. My job was to go there to collect it, and after a very short time I became deeply concerned when I saw the products of the abbatoir in butchers' shops. In that disgusting place I witnessed terror, panic and animals screaming, and I will never forget seeing a cow decapitated and watching her eyes still rolling round in her head some time afterwards. I even saw animals lying with their throats cut, left to bleed to death.

Years passed. I went to drama school, where I met Jean, and then came seasons of acting in repertory companies all around the country, when there was little time to devote to anything other than learning parts and basic living. But when we were in our late twenties, we both decided to give up eating meat and some years later, having searched our consciences and given serious thought to the human/animal relationship, we became vegans, avoiding not only animal foods, but also dependence on wool, leather and all animal products. Today we share our home with three dogs and two cats and we can look all of them straight in the eye.

I am of the opinion that animals have far greater intelligence than we recognise. The discovery that whales can talk to each other over great distances was a big surprise to the world, porpoises and dolphins suddenly became intelligent creatures and the public became greatly interested in learning more about animal culture through wildlife television programmes.

When we watch our dogs and cats communicate, we are not surprised. They can pass a message with just a look; and likewise pick one up from us. Jean and I may be talking in quite normal tones, saying, for instance, what a lovely day it is and wishing we didn't have to work, because then we could be out in the sunshine. One of our dogs, ever watchful, will either catch the word 'out', or perhaps, for its own convenience, will wilfully interpret our mood of wishfulness into one of deliberate intent. The dog will look at the rest – and that is that! They all pile on top of us with loud barks of canine delight . . . *we're going out, we're going out*! And so, of course, we do.

Animals also know the difference between right and wrong, and will act a lie without any shame. Everybody has known the dog who pretends to swallow a tablet then spits it out and covers it with a paw to hide the evidence; and one of ours, Becky, developed a most cunning ploy. She discovered that if she went running out into the garden at mealtimes, barking loud messages of excitement and alarm, William would instantly leave his dinner and go tearing out after her. While he was roaring up and down the fence, view-hallooing like a Millwall supporter, Becky would smartly double-back, nip indoors and start wolfing down his dinner. . . . unfortunately for her, William ultimately got wise!

Our three dogs are William, seven, Becky, five, and Gussie, two, who was bought from a local pet shop. We had gone in to buy food for William and Becky and saw this pathetic scrap in a kind of bin, the last unsold of a litter. She had to come home with us. Becky took her into her basket and tried to mother her, but no sooner had they cuddled down together than Gussie would bite her, trying to find her nipples and Becky would leap out in anger.

We originally had a tabby cat, which, sadly, was run over and killed. A while back, the Cats Protection League asked us to look after a white cat over Christmas for somebody who was going away. We welcomed her, but shortly after her arrival she gave birth to two kittens. The mother went back in the new year, but we kept the kittens, two fluffy little white objects, one of whom is totally deaf. Right from the start all the dogs accepted and adopted them.

Nowadays we get up at 5.45 a.m., and before I go off to the studio we spend an hour and a half exercising the dogs, playing in the woods and fields. The problem of keeping the cats happy and healthy in a traffic-laden area was solved by erecting a large cat run in the garden. They spend the day alternately demanding to go out into the cat run, come back in from the cat run, go back out to the cat run. . . . White cats, even deaf ones, have peculiarly penetrating voices. We are never in any doubt as to their wishes! And, needless to say, we drop everything to minister to them. You don't keep a cat waiting.

We both feel deeply and strongly about the way animals are treated by the human race. They are legally abused in laboratories, abattoirs, circuses, batteries and many other areas, and they have no voice whatsoever. I cannot envisage any healthy animal that wishes to die or to be used for experiments or to be forced to perform tricks for the enjoyment of man, and yet they must submit to our wishes without complaint or redress.

By giving up any reliance on the products which animals are forced to provide, we can live with our own consciences. We also try in every way possible to support those who dedicate their life's efforts to the improvement of the lot of animals. However, so long as man regards himself as master of the planet, I see little hope for the lesser species. As a race, I fear we are on the road to destroying the environment on which many species depend, and in the process we may well destroy ourselves.

25
DOGS COUNT TOO!
An interview with Colonel Anthony Hare

Colonel Anthony Hare was educated at Radley College and the Royal Military Academy, Sandhurst, and served in the Army for thirty years before taking up a second career in the National Health Service.

Married, with three children, Colonel Hare is a natural animal lover who was thrown in at the deep end when he became Director General of the Battersea Dogs Home in 1988.

'Dogs count too!' That was the slogan we adopted when the Battersea Dogs Home took part, for the first time, in the Lord Mayor's Show last year. The theme of the new Lord Mayor was 'People Count', and we thought ours was a timely reminder to the people of London.

Dogs are our foremost animal companion and there is no denying the bond which inevitably grows between owner and pet. I have always had a dog – always a black labrador, for no particular reason – and during my Army service the dog always accompanied my wife and myself wherever I was posted. We went together to Germany, Cyprus and Malaya, and despite the separation of quarantine and the unsuitability of some overseas climates, I am sure that neither we nor the dog would have had it any other way. When I joined the Battersea Dogs Home there was a yellow labrador here and we were very happy to give her a home, so now we have two.

Before I was appointed Director General early in 1988, I had little idea of the enormity of the stray dog problem in London. Over twenty thousand dogs pass through this home alone in an average year, and only about thirteen per cent are reclaimed by their owners. For a nation of so-called animal lovers this is surely a sad indictment. Fortunately, uncaring people are matched by those who do care. And the staff at Battersea care too.

Evidence of this was shown in an incident shortly after my arrival. Two dogs came in together as strays on the same day – Fleetway was a six-year-old mongrel and Duke was a cross labrador aged about ten months. They were both in the same sales pen when two couples came to view. After the usual interview, both were awarded the dog they had chosen; Duke went to the couple with a young family and Fleetway to the others, who lived in Knightsbridge.

Within twenty-four hours Fleetway got out and was seen near the home, allegedly trying to get back in. Staff tried to catch him, but he disappeared again, only to be heard trying to get in again later that evening. The next day he was picked up by the British Rail police at Clapham Junction station and returned to Battersea. The staff were convinced he was looking for his pal Duke, so I rang the owners of both the dogs to see if one of them would contemplate having the two of them together. We arranged a meeting in Hyde Park – owners and dogs together – but no agreement could be reached, so we were back at square one.

Some time later, Duke's owner brought her dog back as he would not settle down, and our reception staff, mindful of the history, reported his return to me. I rang Fleetway's mistress again, only to find that she had now acquired a companion for him. A new and happy home was found for Duke, but this incident has remained in my mind as an example of the interest in the individual dog shown by our staff, when we sometimes have as many as six or seven hundred in the home at one time.

I would like to dispel a popular misconception. A great many people imagine that unclaimed and unsold dogs at Battersea are put down after seven days. This is completely untrue and probably emanates from the fact that the Metropolitan Police pay the cost of the first seven days for dogs collected from police stations. In fact, no dog is ever destroyed unless there is good cause, such as extreme age, severe illness or temperamental unsuitability. Otherwise unclaimed dogs are sold, and that is why the home is overcrowded.

Another interesting aspect is the way in which dogs are sold to the public. They are priced at anything between twenty-five and fifty pounds according to breed, age and fitness, and around thirty are sold on an average weekday and seventy on a Saturday. However, applicants are carefully vetted by qualified staff. A questionnaire has to be completed, followed by an interview, and if we have any doubt about the suitability of the home offered, a call by one of our home visitors is arranged prior to taking a decision.

All this would be meaningless unless dogs offered for sale were guaranteed fit. Under the direction of the home's Manager and Veterinary Surgeon, Bill Wadman-Taylor, every new arrival is given an injection and spends the first seven days in quarantine. Every outgoing dog has a certificate of health, and any purchaser who brings back a dog within seven days, for any reason, has their money returned.

Stories of Battersea dogs are legion, and so are those of former owners, who include some of the more colourful members of society, even short-term prisoners! Some years ago a mongrel dog was found at Charing Cross station, sitting on guard over a pair of shoes. Neither police nor station staff could part him from them and when he was finally removed by staff from Battersea, they had to take his lost master's shoes along as well. He was named Bootsie and went to live with a lady in Bristol, with whom he enjoyed eight happy years.

Dogs are very perceptive and many have found affection and care at Battersea for the first time. It is not unknown for reclaimed or sold dogs to find their way back again, and one particular dog has gone down in the history of the home on this count. Blackie was his name; three times he was sold to a good home and three times he ran away and returned to Battersea, asking to be let in. Finally he was allowed to stay and remained in the permanent charge of a friendly kennelmaid.

The sad side of the story, so continually evident to all of us who are involved, is the yearly increase in the number of stray dogs picked up on the streets of London. Battersea is about to build two hundred new kennels and we intend to use our satellite kennels at Old Windsor for selling Battersea dogs. We face a continuing battle to compete with the needs of the rescue operation and it is a great pity that there is such callous disregard for the welfare of what we laughingly call man's best friend.

26
A STRANGE DINNER PARTY
by Tippi Hedren

Tippi Hedren is best known as the star of the Hitchcock films
Marnie *and* The Birds. *However, she later gave up her film
career to make a film with her husband about African wildlife, a
decision which led to the devotion of her life to big cats, the lions
and tigers which now share her nature reserve home in California.*

The star of the following extract from Tippi Hedren's book The
Cats of Shambala *is Neil, a lion born in Africa and brought to
the United States as a young adult. In order to familiarise Neil
with Tippi, her husband Noel and her family before filming, his
trainer Ron introduced him into their house as a daily visitor. The
social consequences make fascinating reading.*

With a full-grown lion in the house, I suppose we should have
expected friends, even close ones, to react with apprehension
to our new acquaintance. Film producer-director Ted Post,
one of Noel's clients and a longtime friend, absolutely refused
to come to dinner unless we guaranteed that Neil would not
drop by. Several other friends made flimsy excuses during this
period and consequently missed some novel entertainment.
But there were also those who took Neil completely in stride.

I anticipated that Emily Henderson would tighten up a little
and show the usual mixture of awe and fear the first time she
met Neil. Instead a wide smile crossed her face. I did feel a
little strange saying, 'Emily, this is Neil.' Yet I also felt that
a formal introduction to an adult lion was necessary. The
human, I've found, needs a bit of a bridge to the big cats.

Despite all the social mixing with our family and his easy
at-homeness, Neil soon proved that he remained very much

beast. An editor at *Life* magazine heard we were learning about big cats in preparation for a movie and proposed a photo essay. For one shot he wanted the Marshall family at dinner, with the live-in lion seated on the landing, gazing down at the humans as they ate their broiled chicken.

We set the scene carefully with polished silver and cutglass stemware, flowers and Wedgwood china on the dinner table. And Noel and I, Jerry, Joel and Melanie (John had a special assignment) gussied ourselves up to look like the California family beautiful. With any luck, the picture would be just right for *Life*.

After we were seated, candles glowing, photographer Mike Rougier began snapping away while middle son John, hidden up on the landing, fed bits of meat to keep Neil interested and *in place*. But Neil kept turning his head and didn't have quite the rapt look that *Life* required. After thirty or so clicks, the camera had to be reloaded. That was the way the magazine worked. Zillions of pictures to get one. John stopped issuing the meat tidbits, and everyone relaxed.

Except Neil. He did what his animal dictates told him to do – go get the food. All four hundred pounds of him leaped smoothly over the railing and landed in the middle of Wedgwood and flowers and cashew chicken. The table hung on two legs for a few seconds, balancing as if on a high wire, then tipped over as Neil made another graceful bound into the centre of the room.

My first reaction was to yell to Mike, 'Did you get the picture?' My second was to bemoan the broken china and stemware and the chicken, rice and salad all over my rug and me. The *Life* people packed up and went home, Rougier thoroughly disgusted because he thought he hadn't got the shot. But a second camera on a tripod had tripped automatically, catching the uninvited diner on the teetering table and the looks of shock on the faces of the humans.

Only Ron was not surprised by Neil's behaviour. He told me it was useless to rebuke a big cat or attempt to teach it any manners it did not wish to learn. So, with our dinner table in ruins, Ron just shrugged and took Neil out to the green van. The lesson was for the humans: Don't leave food on the table when a lion is near.

About a week later, on another of the evenings when Neil visited, we had several BOAC public-relations people in for dinner and they were, understandably, quite anxious for a few minutes. We had not warned them that a friendly big cat might come through the door at any minute. Stiffly British about it all when Neil did appear, they forced squeaky little laughs and stood rigidly until they realised that he was not planning to make an evening meal of them.

Yet we soon saw the ultimate unpredictability of the big cats. Later that evening Neil suddenly became *possessive*, one of the most dangerous situations that can develop. It came on without warning, and, so far as could be determined, it was over Ron himself. Neil apparently did not want Ron sharing his attention with others that night. Growling deep in his belly, he began to display aggressiveness, baring his canines, lifting a paw. In a few seconds, he went from friendly lion to terrifying lion right there in the confines of our kitchen.

We had heard about the possessive traits of the big cats, which are predictable. Totally unpredictable are the moments they may choose to display those traits – and the object they choose to possess. Neil wanted Ron, and he was threatening both of us.

'Get out of here,' Ron shouted to me, and I ran into the living room, where Noel and all the guests were on their feet, several edging toward the front door.

It was the first time I'd seen a demonstration of possessiveness, and my first lion – human encounter except those staged in circuses with cracking whips and chains. This one wasn't staged. And we were all scared, witnessing the showdown between Ron and Neil from about forty feet away, through the open kitchen door.

Neil's tail was twitching and one huge paw was batting the air. His mouth was open, lips pulled back, and he wasn't grimacing. Shining canines were exposed. Snarls came from deep in his throat, choppy and hoarse. I remembered what

Ozzie Bristow had said about Dandylion: 'He loves me, but he could also kill me.' Neil had reverted to raw jungle.

Ron, yelling, 'No! No! No! Leave it,' was facing him down. Less than three feet separated them. Ron's hands and arms were raised threateningly. They were his only weapons, symbols of some larger threat. *He had to win*! The trainer *must* win the fight, we learned that night. It was a chilling lesson for the future. If the big cat wins, the relationship has to be ended for the sake of the human.

Though it seemed to last for an hour, it was probably no more than two minutes before Neil tossed his head and mane in surrender, then began making subdued muttering noises. The big mouth relaxed finally; the paw went back on the floor. A moment after that, an embarrassed Ron Oxley was escorting Neil out to the van.

As I closed the door behind him, I heard Ron talking to the lion as one would admonish a brat: 'They're nice people. Why did you act like that?' It was useless admonishment and Ron knew it.

We quickly poured some potent drinks for our guests, but it was a few more minutes before confident laughter could be heard in the house. Stiff upper lips had been tested all around.

About a week later, we were treated to another display of possessiveness. We were out in Soledad Canyon, at Steve Martin's place, with the same group of BOAC public-relations people, working with Boomer, a two-year-old lion belonging to Martin. In very late afternoon Boomer was being photographed carrying a BOAC flight bag in his mouth. Trouble began when he decided he wanted the bag. Belly on the ground, prize between his teeth, Boomer was ready for an all-night stand until Ron hooked a rope to the bumper of his van and literally towed the lion, bag still in his mouth, back to his quarters.

More than anything else, I think it was that stunning combination of lovable lion and raging beast all in the same beautiful body that became a fatal attraction for me. The lovable lion always melts the heart; the raging beast terrifies the head.

27
ANIMALS AND THE CAMERA
An interview with Marc Henrie

Marc Henrie is one of our leading animal photographers, and a 'natural', having almost been born with a camera in his hand. After seven years in Hollywood, meeting and photographing famous film stars and their animals, he returned to his home country to concentrate on working with cats and dogs. His reminiscences and observations reveal his deep understanding of what he regards as 'the little people'.

I was eight and a half years old when a national newspaper first published one of my pictures. My father was a keen amateur photographer, specialising in wildlife pictures, and on my eighth birthday he bought me a box Brownie camera so that I could learn to share his interest. One day, in the local park, I saw a nun sitting on a bench with a pigeon on her shoulder, so I took a picture of the scene and my father developed it and made an enlarged print. He knew someone on the *News Chronicle*, then a leading newspaper, and they published it. That set me on the road.

We had dogs and cats, which I began to photograph. My father was sufficiently pleased to buy me a better camera, and in the next few years, with my third and even better camera, I was much in demand by friends and neighbours and built up quite a local reputation. Up till then I was always paid in sweets, but as the work increased, my father said I must start taking money instead, as the sweets were ruining my figure!

My mother wanted me to go into law or medicine, but my family has always been connected with the film industry. An uncle of mine had gone out to Hollywood in the early days and joined up with Mack Sennett, and I had a feeling I should follow the same road. So at sixteen I became apprenticed to Gainsborough Studios at Islington. I began as a general dogsbody, sweeping out, then they let me mix chemicals, and eventually I was allowed to hand the film up to the chief photographer. In those days stills were photographed in special studios, with portrait sessions for the artistes. When stills of selected sequences were required during shooting, the action stopped, everybody froze and the stills man appeared, with his stand camera and big plates, to take a couple of shots, after which the shooting resumed.

So it was that after three years I was judged competent to try my hand. I well remember the first picture I took. It was of Patricia Roc, and she was very kind and helpful. Soon afterwards I went to work at Bray Studios for a short time, but the film industry here never had the charisma of Hollywood, so I wrote to my uncle, who offered to support me for a few months while I looked around. A test with RKO was successful and I became a humble Number Four stills man, the lowest form of life in the studio. I progressed, with experience, and stayed for seven years, during which I met and photographed many of the stars, like Edward G. Robinson and Marilyn Monroe. A colleague and I were the last people to photograph Marilyn and I still find her death a mystery.

It was in Hollywood that I became recognised as an animal photographer. Gary Cooper had a monkey which he had brought back from a location and he also had a horse. I photographed him in his cowboy outfit on horseback, together with the monkey, and this led to specialisation. Edward G. Robinson had a Siamese cat called Twinkle, Bette Davis and James Cagney both had boxer dogs, and it went from strength to strength.

When I eventually returned to England I decided to concentrate on cats and dogs, with whom I enjoy a special affinity. Cats I find particularly attractive as sitters. I chat to them and we get to know each other, and after these preliminaries the animal is usually receptive and cooperative. I aim to treat my subjects as I did the Hollywood stars. Every dog or cat is a star to me, and I think I have achieved a measure of success with that philosophy.

People who breed dogs and cats professionally are often eccentric, in the nicest possible way. Last year I went to a lady in Essex to photograph a Birman cat and found that she was also a dancing teacher. I had to set up in a corner of the ballroom, and I soon discovered why. Shortly after I had commenced work, the music started and couples appeared on the floor, dancing a waltz. The owner then came over and said, 'Do you dance?' I hastily assured her I was no dancer. 'What a pity!' she replied. 'We are short of a man.' Later, a formation team took the floor, while I was photographing some chinchillas, and again I was asked to break off and take part in the dancing. And once again I protested my inability to dance. 'Then you should learn,' I was advised. 'Perhaps later in the afternoon . . .' It was a chaotic session. The cats, however, loved the music and this helped with the pictures.

Another strange experience occurred when I visited Lord St Oswald in Yorkshire, to do some photography for him. After dinner on the evening of arrival, we all went to our bedrooms. Mine was an enormous room, with bathroom en suite, a huge wardrobe and book-lined walls. I was reading in bed when the wardrobe door suddenly opened, followed by the bathroom door. I shut them both, then they opened again and some books fell on the floor. Finally a cat appeared, disappeared, then reappeared beside me, and I actually stroked it – or thought I did – before it disappeared again. I had been talking during dinner about my interest in psychic phenomena and I wondered if I was the object of some practical joke.

At breakfast next morning I told my host of my strange experience. 'Ah, yes,' he said. 'That was my grandmother's cat, Marmalade. As you were blowing your trumpet at dinner about psychic phenomena, I put you in the haunted room.' It seemed that the cat, Marmalade, had been accidentally shut in the room when the family went away on holiday and the whole house was closed. They returned to find it dead. I still wonder, did I see and stroke it? Whether or not the cat was there, the doors certainly kept opening and books fell about.

Although I do not often work with the big cats, I have photographed lions and tigers in African game reserves and I once went out with a warden to get some shots of tigers in their own habitat. We went out to the same spot again a few days later, and in the meantime the van had been repainted in a different camouflage pattern. When we arrived we were immediately attacked by a lion because the van was no longer familiar and now an enemy.

There is often an element of surprise involved in working with animals. However experienced the photographer may be, however much preparation has been made, the extra special pictures are always the result of the unforeseen. One client had a non-pedigree cat and a small chinchilla kitten. When I was photographing the non-pedigree, which was reclining, the kitten came in and suddenly jumped on to the cat's back – and we had a fantastic picture which could not possibly have been posed.

Photography is an art, like painting; it is a gift which some have. You can be taught the mechanics of taking pictures, just as you can learn how to mix and apply paint, but seeing the resulting photograph in advance is the essence of the art. However, the painter has a distinct advantage over the photographer. If the subject is not looking its best, the painter can put in his own interpretation and even change the background. The photographer cannot, but he captures a moment in time which the artist does not.

My own cats and dogs at home are very special to me. My wife and I brought a kitten back with us from our honeymoon. We named him Fittleworth, the smallest of a litter from a hotel cat. He turned out to be quite a performer and appeared in a number of West End productions, including *Spring and Port Wine* with Alfred Marks. He was in two horror films with Vincent Price, and in his long and distinguished life of nineteen years he took part in about thirty-eight productions and loved it. He even had a photograph and a write-up in *The Times*.

We now have a Cavalier King Charles, the survivor of a pair and aptly named Calamity Jane, and an elderly red and white non-pedigree cat called Topaz. And, to my mind, there is nothing to equal the welcome an animal owner receives on returning home at the end of the day. All worries and frustrations are smoothed away and all seems right with the world again.

28
THE BEARS OF LOCH LOMOND
by Clive Hollands

Educated at St Clement Danes School, London, and St Mary's College, Liverpool, Clive Hollands served in the Royal Navy from 1946 to 1953 and as Marine Personnel Officer for an American tanker company from 1953 to 1966, when he joined the Scottish Society for the Prevention of Vivisection as Assistant Secretary. He is now Director of the Society and Secretary of the St Andrew Animal Fund. A tireless worker for animal causes, Clive Hollands is a member of the Home Secretary's Animal Procedures Committee and of the Farm Animal Welfare Council, both appointments of distinction which reflect his knowledge of animal welfare matters.

It all started with a telephone call from Virginia McKenna, the actress and founder of Zoo Check: 'Clive, is there anything you can do to help save the bears at the Cameron Wildlife Park on Loch Lomondside?'

That telephone call was remarkably similar to one I had some three years earlier from Cyril Rosen of the International Primate Protection League: 'The IPPL has just purchased sixteen stumptailed macaques from Stirling University to prevent them going to another laboratory or being sold to a dealer,' he said, and added: 'They really are Scottish monkeys, Clive, so can you find a home for them?' That call led to the launching by the St Andrew Animal Fund and the Scottish Anti-Vivisection Society of the Scottish Monkey Appeal, a national appeal which raised the necessary funding to provide a new purpose-built permanent home for the colony at Edinburgh Zoo.

However, to return to the bears, a number of factors – including a planned change of use of the site and the inadequacy of the perimeter fencing – had necessitated the closure of the park and removal of the bears. In the winter of 1985, for example, an inspection revealed that some of the bears had dug out hibernating dens which were actually beyond the perimeter fencing.

Once again the St Andrew Animal Fund joined forces with the Scottish Anti-Vivisection Society and the Scottish SPCA in an attempt to find a solution. However, this was a much more difficult problem, for two reasons. Firstly it was a mixed colony comprising North American black bears (*Ursus americanus*), European brown bears (*Ursus arctos*) and Himalayan black bears (*Selenarctos thibetanus*) plus one baby bear, 'Ziggi', which had been reared as a pet.

Secondly, the year was 1985, the time of the Bob Geldof appeal to relieve the suffering in Ethiopia, and it was unlikely that a public appeal to raise funds for the bears would achieve anything like the sum needed.

In spite of efforts by one of the part-owners of the park, the Alloa Brewery Company, to rehouse the bears, the press had a field day – 'Bears before beer protest', 'Trouble bruin', 'Let sleeping bears lie'. The story then started to get out of hand altogether when the baby bear, 'Ziggi', went missing. New headlines in the press: 'Kidnappers grab Ziggi the Bear', 'Campaigners deny kidnapping cub from bear park'. A few days later, 'Ziggi' mysteriously turned up at the park – a mystery which to this day has never been satisfactorily explained.

Back to the main story. Through the good offices of the many people who became involved, eventually the European and North American bears were offered a new home at the Windsor Safari Park, to which they were subsequently moved.

Discussions with the Director of Glasgow Zoo led to an offer of a three-acre wooded valley site for an enclosure for the seven remaining bears. The snag was the cost of boundary fencing, some eight hundred metres of which would be required, together with night dens, a public safety fence beyond the boundary fence and an extension to the zoo's outer perimeter. A staggering hundred thousand pounds was the final estimate. The only thing that was not in short supply was muscle power, which could be supplied from the zoo's very large commitment to the Manpower Services Commission programme.

In spite of the efforts of all concerned, including a most generous offer from the Alloa Brewery to put up thirty thousand pounds towards the new enclosure, it seemed that only a miracle could save the remaining group of bears.

The miracle occurred in the office of Alloa's Managing Director, John Mackenzie. It was a chance remark by one of the brewery's senior staff, who pointed out that in addition to committing this money, they would have to meet the cost of removing the old fencing from the Cameron Park site before it could be redeveloped.

'If we could arrange for the fencing to be cleared from Cameron Park, could we have it for nothing, together with the sum already promised?' I asked. John Mackenzie willingly agreed to the proposal and on that basis Richard O'Grady, the Director of Glasgow Zoo, said yes, they could now go ahead.

We knew the task of removing a mile or so of fencing, twelve metres high and with an overhang above and at least a further metre below ground level, would be a mammoth undertaking, but sufficient material would be salvaged to provide all the fencing required at Glasgow Zoo not only for the boundary fence to the bears' enclosure, but also the zoo's perimeter fence and probably the outer visitors' safety fence.

The bears had to be moved to a temporary home, and thanks are due to Mr Clubb of Clubb-Chipperfield and the Windsor Safari Park for agreeing to house the seven bears until the Glasgow Zoo enclosure was completed.

The Alloa Brewery Black Bear Enclosure was officially opened on Friday, 9 July 1988 by Johnny Morris OBE, the broadcaster and television presenter of 'Animal Magic', and the special plaque acknowledges the help given from many sources and the 'miracle' which made it all possible.

29
ORIENTAL CATS
by Professor Christopher Howe

Christopher Howe has been Professor of Economics with reference to Asia at the University of London since 1979. From 1972 to 1978 he was Head of the Contemporary China Institute, and since 1974 has been a member of the Hong Kong University and Polytechnic Grants Committee.

Married with two children, Professor Howe is the author of a number of books on Chinese economics and lists his recreations as music, gardening and Burmese cats.

ON FINDING ORIENTAL CATS

For most of my pre-college years I lived in West Hampstead, in a large house with a large garden and a very large orange cat. When I moved to my own first house in a small suburban town, it seemed natural to acquire a friend of my own. Having found a house through the local advertiser, a newspaper seemed a likely medium to search for cats. And that was how Joseph Conrad came into our lives.

Six weeks was probably too young to leave birthplace and mother, and as I was out most days, time probably passed rather slowly. Joseph Conrad made up for this by frenetic devotion and excitement in the evenings, during which he would race up and down the carpet until, exhausted, he collapsed on a sofa or in front of a fire. These early experiences probably accounted for the neurotic strain that developed in his behaviour and made the adjustment to the arrival of my wife, some nine months later, that much more difficult. For some time, Joseph Conrad reacted quite unfavourably to this event, not only by thieving whole joints of meat when occasion offered, but also by lying in wait in the airing cupboard on the landing and raining blows on her as she passed by. Eventually, of course, he realised that my wife had more to offer him than anyone, and by the time our daughter arrived, he had become a model of familial virtue.

Some years later, we moved to London and found ourselves with a small, chocolate Burmese. Having concluded that the balanced, happy cat probably needed a friend, I was dispatched to the kennels of a famous Burmese cat breeder in Surrey, who explained to me that all Burmese cats derived from a small group of ancestors in California in the 1940s. This kind lady later sold us Illuskass Rastar, a cream Burmese with a pedigree stuffed with champion forebears. At every stage of his life, Illuskass has been a proud, handsome and much admired cat, although we later changed his name to George. Introducing George to chocolate Julia proved harder than anticipated. George was all for a relationship, but Julia spat at him on first sight. For a week they sat at opposite ends of a room, twenty-seven feet apart initially, but day by day the gap narrowed, until on the seventh day they were found together in a jumbled, loving heap. Although the following years did not maintain this idyllic happiness, there is no doubt that two are happier than one, especially when things are bad and mutual consolation is needed.

LIVING WITH BURMESE

Burmese cats talk, attach themselves strongly to people, and look after children and the sick with infinite devotion. They are fiercely territorial and some are such inveterate fighters that they take unnecessary years off their lives. Joseph Conrad's father was in this mould, as was Joseph Conrad himself. He fought all intruders into his half-acre garden until, at nine years, full of penicillin, he succumbed to a slight illness. Our later cats seem to have learned, to some extent at least, that physical battles are not essential to survival.

Having clear views about the world and what they want from it, Burmese cats are inevitably frustrated from time to time. In these circumstances their revenges are apt, swift and much to be feared. They can also be very expensive. They usually involve the destruction or spoiling of any object which, literally or symbolically, has intervened between you and your duties towards them. A large seventeenth-century Chinese blue and white plate was an early victim of Joseph Conrad. Julia and George are particularly prone to sorting or spraying papers and luggage, which they (quite correctly) associate with lack of attention, abandonment and life at the kennels.

ON PARTING FROM CATS

Finding, living and parting from cats is amusing, stimulating, maddening and, at times, unbearably sad. With Burmese, their intelligence, psychic sensibility and attachment to particular persons make all phases of life with them exceptionally intense and rewarding. When they've gone, memories of them are indelible, and it may well be that they feel the same about us.

30
RACING WITH HUSKIES
by J. Noel Hulmston

*Born in North Wales of an Irish family in 1942, Noel Hulmston
(a law court official in Mold, in Clwyd) has spent a large part of
his life in pursuit of mountain activities. Team Leader of the
Clwyd Rescue Team, he was awarded a Fellowship of the Churchill Trust in 1983 to research transportation and life preservation
in severe winter weather in Alaska and Wisconsin. He has built
up his own team of samoyeds, which is used for training, pleasure
treks and rescue work in the mountains of North Wales.*

*Last year Noel Hulmston became the only British competitor in
a major Swedish dog race, and here he describes how he became
involved in this exciting and gruelling sport.*

Breaking a leg is not the usual way people become involved
with huskies. It was a poignant date, the fourth of July 1981,
American Independence Day, that I lay in a field in Lancashire, my foot trying to disassociate itself from the rest of me.
My arrival in the field had been unceremonious, at the end of
a parachute from an aircraft half a mile above. I had real
doubts as to whether I would ever get back into the hills, let
alone travel on cross-country skis.

A solution to the problem came some nine months later in
Sweden when I met Loda. As dogs go, he was different. Bred
by Lapland reindeer herders, Loda had been given to a friend
in exchange for help with the paperwork, interminable these
days even for reindeer herders. At first glance it was hard to
be precise about his ancestry, but a closer acquaintance left
no room for doubt that this was an intelligent dog. Realisation
dawned upon me that he was also a keen working dog. Staffan

skied along, while Loda towed equipment behind him in a pulka attached by bamboo shafts to a special harness. As I skied along, with my right leg trying to cooperate, my mind began to draw on what I was seeing in Sweden.

Putting things into practice was another matter! First I had to find a dog suitable for work as a sled dog. Enquiries led me to look closely at the samoyed as a potential ally in the cause. Fortune smiled upon me a few weeks later when I saw an advertisement in a South Wales newspaper. One telephone call and I was on my way south. At only a week old, the tiny bundle lay in the corner of a barn; it was hard to judge what I was buying, but buy him I did. I became the proud owner of Twm, although it was a further four months before he travelled to North Wales. In that time he grew into a sturdy young dog with a very definite mind of his own! His early learning experience, competing with other dogs for food in the barn, would eventually stand him in good stead when he became my lead dog. Next thing for me was to find equipment suitable for working a single dog.

In Wales it was difficult to find what I needed, so I solved the problem by making it. Equipment comes for two purposes – training and when it snows. Harness, pulka towing frame, wheeled truck and sled were all duly tested and ready. Peculiar looks became the norm as Twm and I trained on the moor near our home. For his part, Twm seemed to draw on generations of working for man and he loved every minute of it. One thing I knew was that the samoyed was originally a 'pack' animal, having a very close relationship with his or her peers. In Twm's case I did wonder whether he was lonely.

Coincidence played its hand just then as two friends asked me whether I would like to have their samoyed bitch. I jumped at the chance and Maja moved in. A far better fate for her than being shot for chasing sheep on the moor where she lived! If dogs could vocalise their happiness then I am certain that this pair would have done so with gusto. Of course, it was only a matter of time before nature blossomed with a pregnancy. Things were looking good; Maja was fit from her work and putting on weight accordingly. She continued to thrive and the due date grew closer.

Eight days before the confinement date there was an explosion in Russia. Not just any explosion, but the holocaust that was the Chernobyl disaster. Of little consequence to me, I thought at the time. Later it became known just how much radioactive material fell on North Wales. Blisters on my wife's neck gave an indication that she had been burnt, but of course she hadn't been, had she? Maja, meanwhile, as my dogs do in the forest, continued to drink from the plentiful rainwater falling in her run.

Birth, when it takes place, is largely out of our hands. In this case literally so; I was in South Wales. The puppies decided to arrive early. Despite valiant efforts by my son and veterinary surgeon, seven out of eight were born dead or died shortly after. One small bitch puppy survived, but that presented a problem. Maja was too distressed to tend her diminutive offspring and I was doubtful about the prospect for survival of this forlorn little creature. Hope came with a home-made incubator and hand rearing. Could it be done? I wondered, as I contemplated the task. I had to try; choice did not come into it. Four times daily, initially with a syringe and later a bottle, feeds were given. She survived and grew into a young dog that seemed to think it was human.

I refused to sell. I like to think this decision was based upon logic, but, in reality, the heart had overcome any logic. Whilst not the biggest or strongest sled dog in the world, Bronwen, as she was named, simply loves to work. No dog could have a bigger heart. Fate once again intervened about then and Sam arrived on the scene. I responded to an advertisement from a Liverpool family which had a samoyed they could not look after. I went to see him. Our first meeting was hilarious; I took a seat anticipating a dog being led into the room. Nothing of the sort happened. A door was opened and a large white mass hurled itself on to my knee, having cleared a settee in the process! He barked at me from a distance of two inches from my nose. What a superb dog he was; I bought him instantly.

Like Bronwen, he too loves to work and is only really happy when working in the hills. The way in which, as an adult dog, he adapted to his role, speaks volumes on the willing nature of these dogs. The team of four worked well together, and towards the end of 1987 I received an invitation to take part in the Storlien Open Dog Race in Sweden, for which I must have an experienced six-dog team. Fortunately I was able to borrow a team from a professional Swedish dog driver, and accepted the invitation with enthusiasm.

Any overseas sporting activity takes planning and finance. Without the practical support of my family and many friends, I would never have made the starting line. There is much talk these days about hype in sporting events, and this came over to me as we waited for the 'off'. It also affected my team as they heard the seconds bleep away. Five, four, three, two, one, and away we went. They had learnt to cope well with a driver who had a funny accent, and they knew that they were stuck with me. My faith that they would reach the finish was based upon their background of working with tourists. They had the experience, which I was perhaps lacking, and the stamina. The race took three days and covered one hundred and twenty kilometres through the mountains; during that time we were self-contained, with all our own gear and food.

Each night saw us at a compulsory camp where competitors must stay, in which a genuine camaraderie exists between everyone, whether top mushers or not. Ambient temperature was a pleasant ten to fifteen degrees below zero, ideal for the dogs. Our nights were only briefly interrupted by the odd howl, as dogs and humans alike recovered from their daily exertions. A funny sort of bond grows between dogs and driver when you rely on each other. In my particular instance I could feel the trust develop in this special bond.

Through no fault of the team, on one occasion I was decanted into the snow and to this day I am convinced that each of my six dogs looked to see if I was OK, perhaps to enjoy the spectacle!

All too soon the last day got under way and we raced with teams from the other classes converging around us, out of the mist, heading for the finish. Breaks in the low clouds enabled a stocktaking as the last few miles approached. My dogs knew that it was the moment to go for the line, and go they did. From the outset I knew I would not be the winner, but my praise for my six could not have been greater even if we had crossed the line first.

As I drank warm currant juice, I had the first chance for three days to reflect. My team of six huskies had brought me safely to the finish. Away to the south the sun shone on the summit of Sylarna, making it sparkle. At just under six thousand feet, it is the high point of the mountains astride the Norwegian-Swedish border. It was an appropriate area for my first race; after all, it was where it had all begun six years earlier.

It has been an amazing six years in which I have built up a continuing bond with my own team. They enjoy their work and I enjoy having the privilege of being able to work them. They have also taught me a considerable amount about myself, for which I am grateful.

31

COFFEEBEAN THE GOAT

by Colonel Ronald Kaulback OBE

Now in his eighties, Ronald Kaulback can look back on a life of great variety. As a zoologist, he explored in Assam, Tibet and Burma. As a soldier, he was Chief Instructor at the Small Arms School in the early years of the 1939–45 war, before returning to Burma with his own command. Latterly he spent thirty years as a hotelier on the west coast of Ireland, where he also studied the marine wildlife. Despite his wealth of experience of animals in many parts of the world, Colonel Kaulback has chosen to remember a much loved childhood pet and an incident which, he claims, robbed the Church of a potential prelate.

Our father lost an arm in Belgium in 1914 and, when he was passed fit again, he became second-in-command of Catterick Camp, where we lived in a lovely house with stables and paddocks and everything small boys could wish for. In 1916, when my brother Bill was five and I was seven, we were given a nanny goat on condition that we looked after her properly, which we did with joy. We loved that goat dearly, milking her daily, grooming her, taking her from pasture to pasture, and seeing that she had nothing but the freshest of fresh bedding at night. Her name was Cicely Audrey Coffeebean Kaulback, and there is no doubt she was the most thoroughly cherished goat in all Yorkshire – if not in the whole of England. I cannot now remember why we called her Cicely, but Audrey was the name of our governess, a great favourite of ours; and, as for Coffeebean – well, there should be no need to explain that one.

Of the many memories I have of Cicely Audrey Coffeebean

(whom, incidentally, we never referred to by any shorter name), I think two are worth recording.

Of course, if our beloved goat were to continue to give us milk, there had to be a yearly visit from a gentleman goat; and, on the first occasion, it fell to my brother to fetch this shaggy and evil-smelling animal from a nearby farm. On the way back they met a couple of young officers who had the temerity to mock our William a little. 'Hullo, Bill,' they said, 'and how much milk does your billy goat give?' Even at five, Bill was a hard nut to crack. He regarded them balefully for a few seconds and replied, with withering scorn: 'How much milk do *your* men friends give?' – leaving the opposition speechless.

As was the custom in those far-off days, children went to Sunday school, and Bill and I were no exceptions. We slept in one room, he and I, with beds close together, and one Sunday night, after we had been put to bed and left to go to sleep, I reminded him that it said in the prayer book '. . . and hath promised, when two or three are gathered together in Thy name, Thou wilt grant their requests'. Bill remembered perfectly and agreed that there could be no misunderstanding such a plain and simple statement. 'Well then,' I continued, 'we're two, and if we kneel up in bed and put our hands together, we can tell Jesus we're gathered together in His name, and we can request that Cicely Audrey Coffeebean be able to speak.' No sooner said than done, and we spent what seemed to be a very long time kneeling and praying most earnestly for this small miracle, certain our request would be granted, because that's what it said. Next morning we dashed to the stall, in perfect faith that we should get a cheery greeting from C.A.C. We were so shattered by the hideous letdown that it was literally years before we were able to believe in anything religious at all. Sad, really, because up till then I had been determined to be a bishop.

32
BEN AND TINY –
THE SQUIRREL MONKEYS
by Greg Knight MP

A Leicestershire man, Greg Knight has always been an ardent worker for the Conservative Party. Chairman of Leicester Young Conservatives at the age of twenty-one, he became a member of Leicestershire County Council from 1977 to 1983, when he entered Parliament as Member for Derby North. Animal welfare rates high among his personal and Parliamentary interests.

It was W. S. Gilbert who said: 'Man however well behaved, at best is only a monkey shaved.'

For centuries man has been both fascinated and amused by our closest relatives.

The keeping of monkeys as pets was very popular in Victorian times, but these days monkey owners are regarded as being rather eccentric. I should know. Just over eight years ago, I came across two young squirrel monkeys in need of a home and I readily obliged.

Of course, you do not need to be eccentric to keep a simian pet, but you certainly need to have a lot of patience and be prepared to devote a lot of time to these highly intelligent animals. Quite simply, monkeys are not easy pets to keep. They need space, companionship, in most cases heated quarters, and a balanced diet. Also, unlike a cat or dog, a monkey cannot be house-trained. In addition, as nowhere is out of reach to a monkey, it is a very risky thing indeed to allow one to roam loose in the home without supervision, as a friend of mine found out to his cost when cups, saucers, plates and bottles were gleefully thrown on the floor by a young monkey having a great time.

However, despite these onerous requirements, keeping a monkey is a rewarding experience. Indeed, the similarity between simian and human behaviour can at times be disconcerting.

No one who has owned a monkey will ever accuse the animal of being obedient. One of the delights and also infuriating aspects of owning a primate is that they behave like naughty children. The relationship between man and monkey can be close, but is never one of master and servant.

Despite their cheeky behaviour, most monkeys are nervous. The first day I took my monkeys, Ben and Tiny, home, they kept a reasonable distance from me until we got to know each other over the next few days. They delighted in exploring each room of the house and on one occasion caused utter consternation by leaping from the top of the lounge curtains on to a large potted plant which was near the fireplace. The monkeys, quite naturally, assumed that the plant – like its wild counterparts – was properly planted and would therefore hold their weight. Unfortunately, the size of the plant pot, although big enough for the plant, was not sufficient also to balance the weight of two leaping monkeys. As a consequence, the whole lot tipped over, wrecking the plant and tipping soil across the lounge. My two friends looked in amazement at the mess they had caused, as if to say, 'Don't blame us – it was the plant's fault.'

Whilst all this was great fun, up to a point, it does reinforce the fact that monkeys really need their own purpose-built accommodation, which should include an outdoor run. My pets were always welcome in the house when I was present, but this particular incident – together with one or two others – did encourage me to ensure that their own quarters were ready for occupation three days ahead of schedule.

One sometimes reads in the newspaper of monkeys escaping and running away. From my experience, I always wonder whether this is because the monkey is unhappy in its particular environment. Certainly Ben and Tiny were let loose on hundreds of occasions – some deliberate some unintentional – and they never once strayed. Indeed, on most occasions they would return to their own shed after a while, or in the case of Ben, who seemed to have learnt what a door knob was for, I would find him sitting on the door handle of the house waiting for me to let him in.

Owning pet monkeys can also shock and surprise friends and neighbours alike. Tiny used to love running along the length of the clothesline at home and, rather like a trapeze artist, completing a number of loop-the-loops on the way, even if this meant – as it did frequently – she became entangled with the washing.

Ben and Tiny also used to delight in running along my garden fence and then leaping on top of my privet hedge, treating it rather like a trampoline. One particular Christmas, a visitor to my neighbour's house had just returned from a party where the alcohol had been flowing well, and whilst walking under one of my trees, he was surprised to find that his hat was lifted off his head. On looking up, his surprise turned to shock and then to amazement when he saw two monkeys fighting over his headgear. He ran back to his friend's house, only appearing after some ten minutes when his host had convinced him that he was not under the influence. After all, it's not very often that you find monkeys removing your hat in rural England.

Because most people find monkeys attractive, no doubt due to their human-like characteristics, whenever Ben and Tiny were loose in the garden, they would always attract a large audience of children who lived nearby. However, this attractiveness was, prior to 1984, exploited by many seaside photographers in Britain who would use a monkey – usually a squirrel monkey – as a prop to encourage a sale. In a number of cases brought to light, photographers were keeping the monkey working all day, sometimes hurling the monkey on to a child's shoulder so a snap could be taken – and therefore a sale obtained – before the child's parents had time to say no. As a result of this abuse, which was clearly cruel to the monkey and a potential danger to young children (like us, monkeys have moods and can get rather irritable after a few hours of being thrown from one child to another) I initiated a debate in the House of Commons. The debate, entitled 'The mistreatment of monkeys', I am informed, holds the Commons record for attendance at an Adjournment Debate, such was the interest that was generated amongst colleagues.

As a result of the debate, the law was changed, and now a prospective owner needs to obtain a licence before he can keep a simian pet. This will only be granted if the monkey is housed in secure and suitable accommodation. This has the dual effect of protecting the monkey by ensuring that it has adequate space, and protecting the public.

Unfortunately, the Spanish have no such law and, even today, drugged chimps whose teeth have been removed are used and abused by seaside photographers, mainly to relieve foreign tourists of their cash. (Those who, like me, are concerned about this continuing disgrace should make their views known to the Spanish Government and to their Euro MP.)

However, this is not the only area of abuse that exists in 1989. Although monkeys and apes are man's closest relatives, history has shown that the relationship has done the monkey no favours. Over the years, non-human primates have been subjected to the most horrific experiments in man's quest for scientific knowledge.

Meanwhile, those that are left in the wild are facing an uncertain future as man continues to destroy their forest habitat.

If there is a lesson to be learnt from owning a pet – simian or otherwise – it is surely that although man may rule the world, he does not own it. We are, for the time being, the landlords, but there are many other tenants whose existence we should respect and do our best to preserve.

33
THE WONDERFUL GIRAFFE
by Betty Leslie-Melville

Having lived in Africa for over quarter of a century, Betty Leslie-Melville is considered an authority on East Africa and Ethiopia, on both of which she has lectured for the past seventeen years.

She is the first person successfully to raise wild giraffes, who treat her house in Nairobi as their own, and she has written eight books which have captured the imagination of the media, film makers and wildlife enthusiasts all over the world. David Taylor, the vet, says 'she is a remarkable lady who certainly has a way with wildlife'.

In translocating the endangered species of Rothschild giraffe in Kenya to the safety of game parks, some babies were separated from their mothers. No game park was going to give a baby giraffe four bottles of milk each day, so my late husband Jock and I took one of them to our property in Nairobi and raised her.

I was raised in a large American city, and having never been around any animal other than dogs, I was afraid of horses, even cows. So when we got three-month-old Daisy, our first giraffe, who, like all giraffe, was six feet when she was born, and over three hundred pounds, I was terrified of her.

However, Jock had been raised on a farm in Kenya and had no fear of her whatsoever. Since wild animals must imprint (a scientific term for bonding) on someone, Daisy wisely chose him. I was a herd member – I was acceptable, but Jock was her mother. She followed him everywhere, and when he went to work she just stood on the lawn as if she were planted and growing there, even her beloved carrots would not entice her to move – until she saw his car coming in the driveway. Then she would run and put her head in the car and snuggle her head against his, then run around the lawn in glee.

Because she was so miserable when he was away, we took another of the endangered giraffe to keep her company. Our new baby giraffe was only a few weeks old, and because I was used to a giraffe by now and had learned how sweet they are, he imprinted on me. For a year we gave them lots of love and the four bottles of milk each day, and Daisy would suck Jock's thumb and Marlon mine for hours.

We wrote a book about them which was made into a movie. The film company left with us the three giraffe they had captured for the film, so then we had five. And now they are growing up and having babies of their own. We have no fences, they are free to leave any time, but although the males wander off from time to time, the females always stay. They all wear 'lipstick' much of the time because they take carrots from my mouth two or three times a day. This causes some visitors to say with disgust: 'Oh, isn't that unsanitary?' and I always assure them it is – there is no telling what the giraffe may catch. They eat nothing but leaves and their mouths are much cleaner than humans'.

The giraffe, now eighteen feet tall, come when called and put their heads in the upstairs bedroom window in the morning to see who's awake; they have their heads over the lunch table, and they like to sit on the lawn and listen to music. They fill us with wonder. They are so gentle and beautiful – they walk like a slow rolling sea, and have the longest eyelashes in the world, and are as soft as velvet to touch. Giraffe are almost unbearably perfect, and I am in love with them – even though they do destroy every plant and flower in the garden and every vine on the house, which used to be pretty but now looks like Wandsworth prison. What we do now is to offer them whatever it is we are hoping to plant, and plant only what they *don't* eat.

Having become true giraffe junkies, we formed the African Fund for Endangered Wildlife (A FEW) and have just about saved the entire endangered species of Rothschild giraffe. We are now trying to save the highly endangered black rhino, elephant and wild dog.

When my husband Jock died, I was faced with a problem. I did not want to sell the house, nor did I feel like staying there alone, so I decided to invite people going on safari to Kenya to stay at the Giraffe Manor in return for a contribution to A FEW. This has proved very popular; it is a good fundraiser and enables me to introduce many animal lovers to the giraffe.

Why do we save animals? Aside from the fact that like a Van Gogh or Michelangelo, a giraffe (or a rhino or any species of animal) once destroyed can never be recreated; and aside from the fact that we should not, with our arrogance, eliminate other creatures who share this globe with us; and aside from the fact that man's soul can be revivified and filled with joy by seeing animals in their primeval settings or having the domesticated ones as companions; and aside from all the aesthetic considerations – the developing countries need the wildlife for purely economic reasons.

In Kenya, tourism is our largest foreign-exchange earner and provides jobs for literally hundreds of thousands of Africans. A FEW established the first educational nature centre in independent Africa. Each month we bus two thousand five hundred African schoolchildren to the centre – free – to teach them about conservation. Eighty-five per cent of the Africans never see the game. You must have a car to go into a game park, and since their average per capita income is only a hundred and eighty pounds a year, Africans cannot afford a car, and even if they got a ride with someone else, they could not afford the entrance fee. As they cannot afford television or children's books either, and we don't have zoos, how could they learn about animals? So we are teaching the children why the game should not be poached.

Most of them have never seen a giraffe before, and they love them. But then who's ever heard of anyone who doesn't like a giraffe? (However, I am also in love with a warthog named Walter, which people have more difficulty in understanding, but if they got to know him they would love him too because of his great intelligence and charm.)

I have seen many giraffe lying dead with a poisoned arrow through them, poached only for the hair from the tail, which is made into a bracelet and sold for thirty pence. I have seen warthogs dead in terrible snares, poached for their ivory tusks. I have seen elephants dead and headless, beheaded with a buzz saw for the ivory tusks. All for the greed of man.

No animal should be poached or used for cruel experimentation. Animals have rights too. But they cannot speak out for themselves – we, the people who care, are the only ones who can speak for them. And we must, for if we do, loudly enough, then our grandchildren will not have to ask, 'What was a giraffe?'

34
THE FATE OF
THE BLACK RHINO
by Sir Christopher Lever Bt

*Sir Christopher Lever is an authority on many aspects of wildlife
conservation. He is a member of the British Ornithologists' Union
and a Fellow of the Linnean Society; he is also Vice President of
the International Trust for Nature Conservation, a Consultant to
Zoo Check, a council member of the British Trust for Ornithology,
and Chairman of the African Fund for Endangered Wildlife
(UK). Sir Christopher is the author of books on the naturalised
animals of the British Isles and on naturalised mammals and birds
of the world. He writes for us in his capacity as a Trustee and a
Patron of the Rhino Rescue Trust, which works to save the
threatened black rhinoceros in Kenya.*

The black rhinoceros has lived in Africa for over three million
years and was originally established over much of the
continent.

Black rhinos are found from semi-arid savannah, bush, and
thorn scrub to montane cloud-forest and moorland. They are
primarily browsers, eating twigs, leaves and the bark of trees
and bushes with the help of a prehensile upper lip. They have
very poor eyesight but an acute sense of smell and excellent
hearing. When alarmed or ready to charge, they emit a puffing
snort, and despite their size are extremely agile. Females give
birth to a single calf only about every third year, so recruit-
ment to the population is slow.

Since the arrival in Africa of European settlers, the species'
population and distribution have dramatically declined.
Rhinos have been killed mainly for their horns, originally as

hunting trophies; since the 1970s, however, they have come under increasing pressure from gangs of professional Somali poachers armed with automatic weapons, who have hunted them ruthlessly to satisfy the demand for traditional (mainly fever-reducing) medicines in the Far East, and for rhino horn dagger handles in oil-rich North Yemen. Contrary to popular belief, less than one per cent of rhino horn (made of densely matted hair) is used – and this almost exclusively by Gujaratis in western India – as an aphrodisiac.

Another reason for the decline of the rhino is the rapid growth in the human population. At around four per cent per annum Kenya, for example, has the highest growth rate in the world. With increasing reclamation of land for farming and demand for wood as fuel and building material, the rhino's distribution has shrunk dramatically, and within the past three hundred years it has disappeared from much of its former range; it is now confined mainly to isolated pockets in the east and southeast of the continent and in Namibia.

The fall in numbers has been equally dramatic; in 1960 there were believed to be around 100,000 black rhinos in Africa; the latest (1987) estimate is about 3,800 – a drop of 96 per cent.

A black rhino was the first large animal I saw in Africa; soon after my arrival a pair of these magnificent animals emerged from a mud-wallow and, without further ado, charged my vehicle. During the rest of my trip I saw so many more that I did not bother to count them. Now I consider myself fortunate to find one in a fortnight's safari.

In an attempt to stem the disastrous decline in the black rhino population, the Rhino Rescue Charitable Appeal Trust was formed in England in December 1985, under the presidency of HRH Prince Bernhard of the Netherlands; the aim of the Trust is to help the government of Kenya to build fenced sanctuaries for the beleaguered black rhino, whose population in the country had fallen from some 18,000–20,000 in 1970 to about 480 – a decline of over 97 per cent.

In March 1986 an appeal was launched in the House of Lords; this was so successful that within a year sufficient funds had been raised to begin construction of the first sanctuary. The site chosen was the Lake Nakuru National Park in the Rift Valley, northwest of Nairobi.

With financial contributions from other conservation organisations and generous donations of materials and services from elsewhere, work was begun on enclosing the 144 square kilometres park with an electrified fence, with manned guard posts – each equipped with automatic anti-tamper alarms, solar panels to provide electric power, and radio communications – every 15 kilometres.

On either side of the fence and running parallel to it a firebreak has been bulldozed outside the sanctuary and a maintenance road constructed on the inside; within the sanctuary a further sixty kilometres of patrol tracks and bridges have been driven through the bush to provide ease of access to mobile patrols, each of which has been provided with a radio for communication with the Trust's headquarters. Natural water holes have been enlarged, deep bore holes sunk, piped water laid on to drinking troughs, and in addition the Trust has helped to finance the construction of two twelve million gallon dams.

Conservation alone, however, is not enough. To ensure the ultimate success of any project, people – especially children – must be taught to appreciate the value and importance to them of wildlife and natural habitats. To this end, Rhino Rescue is developing its own education programme. This began with talks to schoolchildren visiting Nakuru; these proved so popular that a four-wheel drive vehicle fitted with a television screen will shortly be acquired, which will enable the Trust to visit local schools and show films about African wildlife. Later a generator will be purchased, thus allowing the unit to travel further afield and give film shows to outlying schools.

The Trust has undertaken to fund the major part of the running costs of the Nakuru sanctuary for an initial period of three years, and has installed its own administrator to protect and manage its investment and liaise with the park authorities. It has also committed itself to paying for doubling the size of the rhino sanctuary in the Tsavo (West) National Park and, thanks to a generous donation from the David Shepherd Foundation, has already contributed to the construction of a further sanctuary in the Aberdare National Park.

No account of the campaign to save the black rhino would be complete without mentioning the contributions of such individuals as Dr Esmond Bradley Martin, who is working to abolish the illegal trade in rhino (and elephant) products, and the efforts of Mr Michael Werikhe to raise funds for the rhino by his sponsored walks through Europe and East Africa.

Only eighteen months after the launch of the Rhino Rescue Appeal, the first black rhinos were released in Nakuru. The park is now home to twenty animals (eleven males, eight females and one calf born since the sanctuary formed), and several of the females are believed to be in calf; a further eleven adult females are due to be added shortly. From this breeding nucleus at Nakuru (which is the first rhino sanctuary in a national park in Africa, and which it is estimated can hold at least sixty adult rhinos) the future of the species in Kenya now seems assured. That such a magnificent creature should ever be allowed to disappear from the earth is surely unthinkable.

35
TURTLES IN THE HOUSE
An interview with Julian Lloyd Webber CBE

Julian Lloyd Webber, the celebrated cellist, was educated at University College School, London, and the Royal College of Music. He studied first with Douglas Cameron and then with Pierre Fournier, before making his debut at the Queen Elizabeth Hall in 1972. He has since performed with major orchestras worldwide and made many important recordings.

Julian Lloyd Webber has a number of publications about music to his name and has contributed to musical journals and the national press in the UK, USA, Canada and Australia. His reading of The Elgar Cello Concerto with Sir Yehudi Menuhin was voted 'Best British Classical Recording' at the 1987 British Record Industry Awards.

I have always been interested in reptiles, and especially lizards, which I find strangely beautiful. Unfortunately, it would be neither practical nor kind to keep a lizard as a pet, but turtles seem almost perfect. They are easy to look after, extremely undemanding and make surprisingly good company.

At present I have two, Hoddle and Waddle. This is not, by the way, any reflection on the speed of those two footballing virtuosos (turtles can, in fact, move alarmingly quickly). Before Hoddle and Waddle there were Boosey and Hawkes – and they made fascinating companions. Although not blessed with an abundance of intelligence, they could be taught to relate, and Boosey learned to come back to my hand when I put him on the kitchen floor, indicating it was time to be returned to his tank. Hawkes, however, seemed to possess a somewhat lower IQ and after eleven years decided to eat all the gravel in the tank. It was an experiment he failed to survive.

Turtles enjoy exercise and variety, and mine emerge from their tank for frequent walks around the floor of the kitchen. At one time I had it in mind to develop a tank with sloping approaches, so that they could walk in and out whenever they chose, but somehow this idea never got off the ground.

People are sometimes surprised to learn that turtles – mine, at any rate – like meat and fish and do not eat green vegetables. Hoddle and Waddle particularly enjoy ham, prawns and other types of fish, and – for contrast – they are very keen on cheese. My attention to their diet could possibly have spoiled them, as the so-called packet of 'turtle food' is now a complete non-starter. Provided I remember, when I eat out I ask for a 'turtle bag', and it seems to work quite well. I would call my turtles seasonal eaters. By nature turtles hibernate, but because of the even temperature they enjoy, mine do not. However, their internal mechanism remains the same, with the result that they eat furiously during the summer, while during the winter they can go for weeks at a time without eating anything.

Apart from their culinary tastes, turtles are fairly undemanding. A suitably equipped water tank, lighting and a little warmth are all they ask. Since my work has involved more and more travelling, they have satisfied my need for household pets, and when I go away, they go to stay with my mother. Of course, I would like a cat – a fluffy Birman for preference – but that is not on the cards at present. Cats I especially like, having been brought up with them, but the London flat of a travelling musician is not the best place for one.

I feel very strongly about cruelty and lack of consideration towards animals. Zoos, for instance, vary greatly. When I visited Gerald Durrell's zoo in Jersey, I was greatly impressed by the understanding which had clearly gone into the care of the animals, and the reptile house was the best I have seen. Yet in some zoos I have seen alligators in such restricted conditions that they can barely move.

Having kept turtles for over fourteen years I would not want to be without them – they really make agreeable companions.

36
LIFE WITH LIONS
– AND AFTER
An interview with Virginia McKenna

Virginia McKenna, the award-winning stage and screen actress, needs no introduction to animal lovers, and is internationally acclaimed for her portrayal of Joy Adamson in the film Born Free, in which she co-starred with her husband Bill Travers. Here she tells how that experience changed their lives and resulted in their devoting themselves to the cause of wild animals and to the campaign against thoughtless cruelty to animals in captivity. Virginia McKenna has also written two books, On Playing with Lions *and* Some of My Friends Have Tails.

As a small child I lived in Hampstead, in a maisonette with my father, and we seemed to cram a lot of animals into it – including four dogs and four cats. But my interest in exotic animals began with *Born Free*, which opened up a world about which I previously knew nothing.

Possibly Bill and I were chosen to play the Adamsons in the film because having a married couple on such a difficult and experimental film would eliminate a number of problems. Nobody before had worked with completely untrained lions (we started with two circus lions but they had to be withdrawn as they were so dangerous, and we carried on with lions who had known people at some stage in their lives). The real Elsa had died before the film was planned.

We had twenty-four lions playing various parts in the film and we got to know about nine or ten of them intimately. For ten and a half months we lived with them and came to know and understand them all quite well. George Adamson was our adviser and teacher, and through his example we learned how to behave with the animals.

There were, of course, many unexpected incidents. There was one particular scene in the film where Joy Adamson had gone to Nairobi for a few days, and when she was coming back, Elsa sensed her return – as animals do. The lioness playing the part was required to come out and sit in the road, looking in the direction from which the Land Rover would appear. They shot the scene in the middle of the day, and no way would the lioness sit there in the heat of the sun. She would stay for a few seconds and then move off into the shade of a tree. The director was getting desperate, until they thought of digging a hole in the road and putting George Adamson inside it. He was then covered over with sacking, through which he poked a brush, wiggling it to and fro. The lioness was intrigued and came up to inspect it, and then, as the director called to her, she looked up – and the shot was in the can. A shot which should have taken a few minutes took the best part of a day.

Each day, before filming began at nine o'clock, we used to go out with the lions for two hours to get rid of their surplus energy, stalking, ambushing, playing football, and during those early morning walks we would do things which would be required in the day's filming schedule. Sometimes it would be riding on top of the Land Rover, sometimes inside it, and they especially loved playing football. Like all animals they had their own individual characters.

There are lots of pressures during filming – usually from producers trying to get one more shot in before the end of the day. Occasionally this created problems; the lions would get fed up and make it quite evident they didn't want to do any more. You learned to understand what they were thinking, to anticipate, and if you took no notice – well, it was *your* fault if you got pushed around. We never pay enough attention to the warnings animals give – they're usually very fair about that.

I don't remember Bill or myself getting scratched, but I did have an ankle broken before we started filming. It happened during one of our early morning walks. We were stalking gazelles with two young lions, a male and a female. As we advanced, the gazelles moved further on and the lions kept cuffing our ankles, because Bill and I were still standing upright. So we got down on our hands and knees and crawled along with the lions, who were getting very excited. My knees were getting so sore I thoughtlessly stood up, and the young male, no doubt thinking I was easier than a gazelle, jumped on me. I went down and my ankle snapped. Luckily Bill managed to attract them away from me by dragging his shirt along the ground, a trick he had learned the previous day when he had lured them out of a thicket. This time he dragged it through the grass towards the Land Rover, settled one lion in the back and one on the roof, and came back for me. When I returned to camp with my leg in plaster after two weeks in hospital, I went straight to see my lion friends. I got a wonderful and affectionate welcome. They found my crutches quite intriguing and within moments had carried them off to a corner of the enclosure, leaving me stranded!

Animals share many characteristics with humans, such as protection of their young, and territorial possessiveness. However, I am totally against dressing them up and teaching them unnatural tricks. Finding that amusing is degrading to the animal and to ourselves.

Two years after *Born Free*, Bill decided to make a documentary about the animals we had used in the film and what had become of them afterwards. He called it *The Lions are Free*. Out of all the lions we used, only three escaped from being sent to safari parks or zoos. These were given to George Adamsom for rehabilitation, and were subsequently released into the wild. A deal had already been done to sell the others, which was a great disappointment to us. Two of them went to Whipsnade, and when we went to visit them for the documentary film, they recognised my voice and came to me at the edge of the compound. It was a very emotional and difficult experience. After that, Bill started to produce and write wildlife documentaries. One of his films was *Bloody Ivory*, about elephant poaching in Kenya. With the documentaries, writing articles and books, we became increasingly absorbed with wildlife issues.

In 1984, spurred on by the untimely and unnecessary death of Pole Pole, a young elephant in London Zoo – an elephant Bill and I had worked with in a film in Kenya in 1968 – and the considerable reaction from both the media and the public, we founded Zoo Check. Today our energies are mainly directed towards investigating and improving the condition of animals already in captivity and emphasising the vital need for genuine conservation – the preservation of wildlife in its natural habitat.

Man's need to dominate other species, rather than coexist with them, appears undiminished. Perhaps in order to justify that somewhat dubious need, people who keep animals in captivity for commercial reasons tell the public we can't really understand or appreciate animals unless we see them in the flesh. I question that. Are they saying we have the right to see everything – whatever the cost to the animal?

Unfortunately, some endangered species – made so by the destruction of their habitat by man – now have to be protected in an artificial way. But a large sanctuary in the animals' own environment rather than as part of a zoological collection would be a more humane and effective way to achieve this. The sanctuary can contain a balanced ecosystem; the zoo compound cannot. Where this kind of conservation is impossible, the alternative should be of the highest quality – recreating, as closely as possible, the animals' social and environmental background.

Zoo Check has just completed a European survey of zoos, a year's work part-funded by the EEC. Over a thousand zoos have been discovered – over twice as many as are officially on record. The problems that have been revealed make a mockery of the position most zoos claim to hold as champions of conservation and education. Solitary elephants, demented bears and chimps do nothing for either – and as far as understanding is concerned, we have wonderful television documentaries about animals and nature, allowing us to observe natural behaviour in its proper setting.

We recently went to Tunis, following complaints to us from members of the public. There is a zoo in Tozeur in which a bear is kept starving, while the guide, taking his visitors around, taunts the bear with little pieces of bread, saying 'No, these are not for you, they are for the visitors'. We saw the bear, with his front legs outstretched, actually crying! There was also a chained camel being fed with Coca-Cola out of a bottle for the amusement of the visitors, who were mostly European, and in another zoo a polar bear was lying exhausted in a temperature of forty-five degrees centigrade. Our investigating team was appalled. They visited four zoos altogether. On their return, we sent an illustrated report to all travel agents who send people to Tunis (and all the Tunisian ambassadors to countries whose nationals were observed at the zoo) asking that the Tunisian zoos should not be part of their sightseeing trips. The response from several travel companies has been encouraging and supportive, and we are hopeful that our continuing work on this issue will bring about significant changes.

It would be unrealistic to expect zoos to cease to exist, but already some of the worst have closed and the animals sent to other 'collections'. Meanwhile, I will always be haunted by what I have seen – the bear in an indoor cage four metres by three; birds unable to fly; the lone monkey chained in its concrete pen. I cannot forget the look in their eyes. It is a look which will follow me for the rest of my days.

37
HIGHLAND PONIES
An interview with Baroness Masham of Ilton

Lady Masham was created a Life Peer in 1970, in recognition of her work on behalf of the disadvantaged. She is President of the North Yorkshire Red Cross and the Yorkshire Association of the Disabled and Chairman of the Spinal Injuries Association.

Brought up with Highland ponies in her Scottish childhood, Lady Masham extended her interest in them after a riding accident in 1958 left her partly paralysed. She has built up a strong breeding establishment at her Yorkshire home and still rides regularly, when her innumerable public duties allow.

My family lived in Caithness, the most northerly corner of Scotland, and as children my sister and I were surrounded by animals. We had ponies, goats and chickens, and we milked the goats ourselves. This was during the 1939–45 war, when Army personnel were billeted on us, and the soldiers used to entice the hens into their tents with tasty food and encourage them to lay eggs for their benefit! We also had guinea fowls, which are very efficient watchdogs. Unlike most birds, they do not sleep at night, but roost up in the trees and raise an alarm at the slightest unusual sound.

Petrol rationing restricted movement, and ponies became our main form of transport and exercise. Highland ponies are very attractive, but they need to be mastered. They are cunning and devious, they will run into trees and throw a rider and try every way to dominate. Nevertheless, they are great fun and have exceedingly good temperaments. They have proved to be good driving ponies and, once they are schooled, can jump and hunt, and can keep going all day. These ponies are also very hardy and, as long as they are well fed and have water, they are happy to live outside, even in the winter.

My childhood fascination with animals did not stop at the ponies which we used to ride and race across the open country. There was a farm nearby and I used to spend my time there in the lambing season, much to the frustration of my governesses, and when I had to go to school I loathed every minute of it.

The accident which changed my life happened in 1958, when I was twenty-two years old. I was staying with some friends in Gloucestershire and was point-to-pointing at the time. I was riding a horse which did not belong to me and it had a warble fly in its back. This results in a hard swelling on the back of the horse, which causes it discomfort, and I have always thought that was why the horse gave an extra jump, fell and rolled on top of me. The horse was unharmed, and up to that point I, too, was extremely lucky, but then another horse, coming up behind us, kicked me in the stomach and I was really fortunate not to be killed. The haemorrhage did not begin until I was safely in hospital, but I then lost a tremendous lot of blood. I was very fit, but I know I only pulled through due to a massive blood transfusion. I spent nine months in hospital and it was my good fortune that my fiancé was nearby, completing his course at the agricultural college at Cirencester. We married in 1959 and have two adopted children.

I am a firm believer in the need to adapt to circumstances, and when we went to live in Yorkshire, I determined to continue riding my Highland ponies, despite my disability. I had a special saddle designed with a built-up back which gives me the necessary support, and I had a pit dug out, into which the pony could walk. This enabled me to mount from my wheelchair and continue to enjoy my riding.

I then decided to start a Highland pony stud at home in Yorkshire. I bought some good foundation stock from Scotland and I had also been given a good mare as a wedding present. I collected various stallions, and over the years I have built up an excellent stud. The stallions, when schooled, are very good in the show ring and one of mine, a yellow dun called Swintondene, has won a number of competitions, competing well against all other breeds of mountain ponies, including the Welsh.

Not all ponies take to trekking, but many Highland ponies seem to enjoy that life. It is all to do with temperament, and some are happier as family ponies with one rider. Their popularity is on the increase and they are now being used in France. It is very encouraging to see that so many people who love Highland ponies are getting such enjoyment out of the many activities for which they can be used.

38
HOW NOT TO BE
A BIRD-WATCHER
by George Mikes

The late Hungarian writer George Mikes is best remembered for his many humorous books in which he observed the quaint habits of his fellow humans in many countries. However, his childhood in a country village also engendered in his inquisitive mind a special interest in birds, which he describes in this extract from his book Tsi Tsa.

I was born in a large village (now a small town) in Hungary, called Siklós. I was surrounded by animals, consequently took no notice of them. There were chickens and geese in our back yard; horses in the streets – motorcars were still such rarities that when we children heard the roar of one, we rushed out to the street to watch. We lived in the centre of Siklós, its Piccadilly Circus, so cows did not go out at dawn and return at dusk with their bells ringing; but cows were, all the same, familiar features of the landscape.

Birds interested me more. We lived bang opposite the Town Hall, which had a clock-tower. On the top of the tower lived, when in residence, a family of storks. I loved those birds, large, beautiful and dignified, and was always pleased to see them arrive. Their arrival meant the arrival of spring, too, of course, but I loved them for their own sake. They were fond of resting for a while on the large fingers of the town clock, pushing them down or else preventing them from rising. The municipal authorities occasionally decided that the face of the clock ought to be covered by glass, but it was never done.

Everybody knew that in the summer the storks made the town clock a little fast (or slow) and that was that.

The storks, as I have said, lived on the Town Hall and they were the guests of the whole community. We, on our own house, had a family of swallows. They came more or less at the same time as the storks, got busy rebuilding or redecorating their nest just under the doorway, brought pieces of mud and other building material in their beaks and later caught beautiful fat flies for their babies. They were part of the landscape, I acknowledged their existence as I acknowledged the existence of chickens and the geese, but was not really interested in them – far less than I was in the storks. When later, in London, I heard the expression *birdwatching*, its meaning had to be explained to me. Who watches birds? And why? And why so early in the morning? When I met my first snail-watcher and saw him crawl around on all fours in a friend's garden for hours on end, I thought he was mad. I still do. I see the point in snail-watcher-watching. But in snail-watching? My father tried to arouse my interest by explaining that the swallows left for Africa in order to get away from our harsh winters, and returned with the good weather. Didn't I think this was wonderful? And didn't I think it miraculous that they could always find our little house in the small village of Siklós? No, I didn't think it miraculous at all. I had an Aristotelian turn of mind and thought in categories. The swallows – as it had been explained to me – were migrating birds. What was so miraculous in migrating birds migrating? It would have been much more miraculous if migrating birds had failed to migrate. And what was so difficult in finding our house? I was a little boy, yet I never had any difficulty in finding it.

I had a painful encounter with a bird and its memory haunted me for years. Perhaps it still does.

I was going home from the Castle – the only historic building of Siklós, where a king had been imprisoned in the fifteenth century – and walking down the hill I noticed that an angry goose was approaching me, followed by a gaggle of goslings. I must have aroused her fear or suspicion – perhaps she was worried about her offspring – and she was coming towards me with determined steps, hissing furiously. I stopped for a moment but she did not; she came nearer and nearer and her hissing sounded more and more menacing. So I decided that we might as well part company. I took to my heels and ran away as fast as I could. The goose – a ferocious animal, smelling blood, and realising that I was afraid of her – started pursuing me, running faster and faster, hissing more and more fiercely. Suddenly I heard loud, mocking laughter. Two little peasant boys were watching the scene and scoffed at my running away from a goose.

For a long time I dreaded the thought that my friends might hear of this inglorious encounter. They never did. My dark secret has been revealed to the world here for the first time.

39

A HIGHLAND BISHOP
AND HIS DONKEY

by The Bishop of Moray, Ross and Caithness

The Rt Rev. George Sessford was born at Aintree, Lancashire, in 1928. Educated at Oulton High and Liverpool Collegiate schools, he graduated with an MA from St Andrews University. He was ordained in 1953 and served as curate of St Mary's Cathedral, Glasgow. In 1955 he was appointed Chaplain to Glasgow University, and after several years as Priest-in-Charge at Cumbernauld New Town, he became Rector of Forres in 1966, and Bishop of Moray, Ross and Caithness in 1970.

Married with three daughters, the Bishop tells how his family life has been influenced over the years by Topsy, the donkey.

It all began with a young priest and a Glasgow brothel! Glasgow in the 1950s had a tough reputation. The Episcopalian Cathedral was situated in an area which had once been genteel, but by the time this young priest was ordained to serve as Curate at the cathedral, there had been major social changes. Many of the tenements had become notorious and there was even a house of ill repute next door to the cathedral.

Unpleasant shocks were frequent for the worshipping public and the priesthood alike, and late one night our young priest was called out to the rescue of a poor woman whose life was being threatened by an assailant. That priest, I must now confess, was myself, and after the police had arrested the man, and the woman was safely in the intensive care ward of the local hospital, I was left literally holding the baby.

That baby, Gerry by name, had been baptised in the cathedral, at his mother's request, on condition that good

Christian godparents could be found who would teach him the faith. The new situation demanded quick action and the next day arrangements were made for Gerry to be taken and admitted to the lovely church orphanage at Aberlour, in the grand Spey valley.

It fell to my lot to see him installed, and a concern to keep in touch with the child led me, with my wife and family, to spend holidays in the Highlands over the following years. Gerry flourished, his mother recovered, her assailant languished in prison and I was moved to Glasgow's overspill town of Cumbernauld, where for the best part of a decade I assisted in building up a new parish.

Then came a second decisive event. My wife had become seriously ill with arthritis and the Highland bishop and the Glasgow bishop together felt that a change of parish would be helpful to her health and our happiness. Thus in the mid 1960s this 'townie' family was translated to a country living in the north of Scotland – and the drama of the donkey began to unfold.

Whilst it was bliss for me and my wife to become Rector and 'first lady' in a small northern town, our three daughters found readjustment a little less easy. Born and bred in city and new town, life in Forres seemed lacking a certain Glaswegian exuberance! In a word, they were bored.

Near Forres there was a school of ballet. The ballet mistress, Veronica Bruce, invited the new Rector and his family over to luncheon one day. Hearing how lonely and bored the three girls felt, she took them out to the nearby donkey stud, which this talented lady ran in addition to the ballet school. Biddy, one of the brood mares, had had a successful honeymoon in Aberdeenshire the previous year and lo and behold, on the very day of the visit of the Rectory family for luncheon, she had dropped her tiny foal.

The children were breathless with excitement. A newborn donkey is, of all creatures, one of the most instantly appealing. With a gait like a Bambi, eyes like a doe, a great dished forehead and fluffy ears, they really are Disney-like in their huggability. Now, beside the Rectory was the garden. The area was large, but the lawn mower small, the grass was high and the Rector was no gardening enthusiast. The children were lonely and, presumably, this donkey would need a new home one day. Could it be that everything was conspiring to pave the way for the entry of a donkey into our lives? Inexorably we were drawn into the affair. If we could care for both mother and foal over the winter – if we would feed and tend them and build them a stable – then, Veronica said, they could live in the Rectory garden and the next spring Biddy could return home (for a second honeymoon) and we could keep the wee one.

The girls were beside themselves. I dashed off to the local forest office and for ten shillings bought a trailerload of offcuts, or 'backs', as the Scottish sawmillers call them – rough planks with the bark still on one side – and before midnight a splendid lean-to shed was nestling in the long grass beside the Rectory garden wall. Two days later the horsebox arrived and the mother and foal were admitted to 'the care of the Holy Church', as one cynical Presbyterian minister put it! Our lives were taken over.

The Rectory dishes had to be washed up in the sink, as the plastic washing-up bowl became the feeding bowl for the donkeys. Mother's wire hairbrush disappeared to emerge as a currycomb in the shed. The leather camera strap was borrowed to make a temporary headstall for the foal. Weekly pocket money was spent on bran and crushed oats instead of ice cream and chocolates – at least until it was discovered that donkeys licked ice-cream cones with great relish, then pocket money had to doubled! A rather more expensive habit was discovered when (I'll not say how) Biddy and her foal exhibited a strong taste for Tartan Special Ale.

By common consent we named the new foal Topsy. It was a highly suitable name in every way – until we discovered that the wife of a local doctor was also called Topsy, and as she, too, was a member of the Episcopal church, we had a few embarrassing moments with that GP. We added the name 'O'Cedar' for two reasons. First, Topsy was of Irish descent and so 'O' rather than 'Mac' seemed a suitable prefix. Second, we discovered that 'O'Cedar' liquid polish worked wonders on her tiny hoofs as we prepared her to take part in the nativity play.

So Topsy O'Cedar became one of the family. Unlike her rather portly mother, Topsy could get through the garden door of the Rectory and she discovered that the mat in front of the study fire was an ideal resting place, though the braying of the frenzied mother for the missing foal always alerted us to her presence.

As befits the occupants of the Rectory garden, both Biddy and Topsy quickly began to exhibit distinctly religious habits. They each had a most lovely black cross on their shoulders – in common with almost all donkeys and, it is said, as a token of their role in bearing our Saviour in Jerusalem on the first Palm Sunday. We first sensed their religious affiliation when an autumn tea-party was held on the lawn and the transistor radio blared out 'Songs of Praise'. Biddy and Topsy were electrified. They came over and ever so quietly and gently brayed in unison with the hymn tunes. We switched the transistor off and they went quiet; switched it on again and they began their accompaniment.

Topsy was brought into the church for the nativity play on her first Christmas but disgraced herself by eating the straw off the roof of the crib as the choir sang 'Away in a Manger' and then dropping unmentionable tokens of her presence on the Sanctuary carpet.

When the time came for Topsy and her mother to be parted, we had moments of great anguish. Biddy was taken straight back to her prospective husband and Topsy left with us. She seemed quite happy and the three girls were out in the garden with her all day to prevent her being too lonely. But at three o'clock in the morning she suddenly discovered two things. First, that her mother had abandoned her and second, that she, too, had lungs and could bray with ear-splitting decibels. Night after night this continued, for more than a week, until we were all bleary-eyed through lack of sleep.

Part of the solution was to leave the gate open between the Rectory garden and the church grounds behind the Lady

Chapel. If Topsy brayed there, the noise did not carry so loudly to the ears of the elders. Alas, before one Sunday evensong, the gate was left open by mistake. Topsy, hearing the organ playing her favourite hymn (just before the sermon), trotted through the open gate and brayed in unison with the hymn. Unfortunately, the organ blower motor was in an adjoining building and when the hymn ended and the sermon started, the blower motor continued to rotate. Topsy, not recognising the difference, went on with her braying, almost drowning my sermon. One rather peppery old colonel, late of the Seaforth Highlanders, who didn't quite approve of the Rector's churchmanship in any case, remarked in a loud aside to his slightly deaf wife, 'There is the other ass braying.'

Forres Gala day was held in the Great Park as usual that year and we entered Topsy O'Cedar in the pets competition. After much consultation – she was neither a dog nor a pony – she was judged in the 'miscellaneous' section. Our daughters were overjoyed when the local vet announced she had won second prize. However, the joy turned a little sour when we discovered that the first prize had gone to an enormous goldfish. I still wonder as to what were the canons of competitive judging between donkey and goldfish!

Four happy years followed at Forres, during which we were privileged to give a home to an ill-used Irish donkey called Simon. In due course Simon and Topsy together produced a delightful chocolate and black foal, which we named Pedro, bringing our equine family to three.

In 1970 the blow fell. I was to be the next Bishop of Moray, Ross and Caithness and so had to leave Forres Rectory and move into the Episcopal Palace (well, actually a mortgaged former greengrocer's town house) in Inverness. It seemed ideal. The Bishop's lawns were large and the greengrocer's outbuildings would have made excellent stables – but we were in the town centre and three donkeys together can make an ear-splitting noise. We reckoned that polite Inverness suburbia might not be quite so forgiving as the long suffering Forresians. . . .

Then the second blow fell. My diocesan registrar (the

Bishop's legal officer) confirmed that a bye-law prohibited the keeping of asses or pigs within the bounds of the Burgh of Inverness. We were devastated. Topsy had to go back to her old home. Veronica generously took her back to the contented life of the Glenerney Donkey Stud, where she could graze in fresh fields and was not deprived of the culture to which she was accustomed. Only now she had to make do with music from the ballet school next door, rather than the church organ and St John's choir!

Simon was a very lively old donkey stallion and would not have fitted into the sedate stud at Glenerney – so he ended up at a nearby distillery. The mash produced by the distilling process proved ideal feeding for him and, alas, he now is not a very good advertisement for Episcopalian and ecclesiastical manners and morals. He is grossly overweight, and to his already randy Irish reputation he has added a distinctly tipsy appearance, due to overindulgence in distillery mash. But the baby, Pedro – that's a different story altogether. He was the only donkey actually bred by the Bishop. Moreover, he had always been surrounded by adoring youngsters. So we sent him off to a nearby good home, to Gordonstoun School, no less. The school chaplain adopted him, so now he is decidedly of the aristocracy, and has even led to his Episcopal breeder gaining an entry in *Who's Who* as pursuing the hobby of donkey breeding.

In a few years' time retirement will come, and with it the search for a home. I have only one absolute condition to lay down. It must be in a place where the local town council does not practise discriminatory legislation against 'asses' – for if the place is not fit for a donkey, it certainly won't do for this Bishop.

40
FRED AND COMPANY
An interview with Nanette Newman

Nanette Newman, actress and writer, has delighted audiences and readers since she first appeared as a child in films for the Children's Film Foundation. Trained at the Italia Conti Stage School and RADA, she starred in a number of successful films and in 1971 won the Variety Club Best Film Actress Award for The Raging Moon, *and the* Evening News *Best Film Actress Award in 1978.*

Television series followed. Nanette Newman has also produced many popular books. She is married to Bryan Forbes, the film producer, director and actor, and they have two daughters.

I have always loved animals, especially dogs, and since I married we have had a succession of dogs and cats, all of which, during their stay with us, have became integrated members of the family. All, that is, except Sam.

Sam, a golden labrador, was a baddie from the word go. He was the most enchanting, naughty dog imaginable, but life with Sam was a nightmare. He would fling himself excitedly at visitors, he would go down to the lake and return, covered in red mud, to jump into an upholstered chair, and he was incredibly greedy, too. Finally Bryan, my husband, decided we must take him to a school for dogs to be properly trained.

We were told of a school whose owner claimed never to have had a failure, which was encouraging. We were assured by the owner that a three-week course would make a new dog of him, which was unbelievable, but we had faith. After three weeks the owner rang to say Sam was, indeed, a quite difficult dog, and might he keep him for an extra week. After the fifth week the harassed owner, almost a nervous wreck, pleaded with us to take Sam away as he was a disruptive influence on all the other dogs.

Sam returned home, as monstrous as ever and just as undisciplined as before. That evening we had some friends to dinner and they brought us a box of chocolates. When we had said goodbye to them we found Sam had eaten not only all the chocolates, but the box as well! The following morning he was lying in his basket looking decidedly unwell, which was hardly surprising. And then I noticed a kind of lump on his shoulder. We took him to the vet, who X-rayed him. The mystery was solved. The previous night we had had meat on skewers for dinner and Sam had swallowed one whole. An operation had to be performed to remove it and he created medical history as it had gone right down his throat and into his stomach without causing any internal damage.

I collected him, and he looked so pathetic with his stomach all sewn up that I felt sorry I had scolded him for eating the chocolates. But sympathy was wasted on Sam; soon after his return home, he stole and ate four steaks and a whole loaf of bread.

Sam adored my small daughter, who was just old enough to walk. He would bound up and knock her over in his demonstration of affection, and one day she fell and chipped a tooth. That was the final straw. Sam had to go. We gave him to a friend who had a farm. He remained untrainable but still lovable. I must confess that all our dogs have been rather badly behaved and I am not sure that we are best qualified as pet owners. Bryan, when he was young, had a pet pig who followed him everywhere on the farm where his family lived. A recent reminder of this occurred when our younger daughter, Emma, adopted a pig under the scheme at the London Zoo – in memory of her father's childhood friend.

I believe that however many animals a family may have over the years, there is always one whose memory remains the most precious. For us, that was our dog Fred. He was rather a mixture, mostly Yorkshire terrier but unusually large for the breed. We had two dogs at that time, and Fred hated the other one. He also despised the cats and completely ignored them, but they were equal to it and returned the compliment.

Fred was with us for a long life and was a wonderful character (he also appeared in two of Bryan's films), but when he was around eleven years of age, he became very ill. We tried to keep him even as he went downhill, dreading the thought of losing him, until our vet finally pointed out that Fred was clearly in pain, unable to enjoy life any longer, and should be put down.

The decision was made, but we asked the vet to come and give the injection at home. That morning the sun shone and the garden door was open. Fred could hardly walk, but he suddenly dragged himself outside on to the lawn and lay down. The four cats then came out, one by one, and gathered round him. They licked him and moved around him for a few minutes and then slowly walked away. It was just as if they had come to say goodbye. Fred then got up and came back into the house, where the vet was waiting.

We now have four cats and we are visited, quite unofficially, by wild and lovely creatures. There is a badger from a nearby sett who comes to our back door in the evening and asks for food. He loves honey and peanuts. Another visitor is a fox, whom we frequently observe sitting in the garden in close proximity to the cats and, clearly, with their agreement. He will pick up the cats' food dish and carry it away into the rhododendrons, where I have to retrieve it next morning. It seems that the news gets around, for lately two pheasants have joined the squirrels in the garden and come to the back door to be fed.

We once had two cats who each had a litter of kittens at the same time. We then had no less than fourteen kittens in the house and we longed to keep them all. But common sense prevailed and we found homes for those we could not keep.

We both love animals and hope that one day, when we don't have to travel quite so much, we can have quite a few. Hopefully not another Sam – but who knows?

41
COME TO THE PARTY
by Lavinia, Duchess of Norfolk CBE

Lord Lieutenant of West Sussex since 1975, when her husband the 16th Duke died, Lavinia, Duchess of Norfolk now lives on the estate at Arundel Park and devotes her life to the many charities of which she is a very active patron. These include the Spastics Society, the NSPCC, Riding for the Disabled and a great number of animal charities, such as the National Canine Defence League, of which she was the first President.

Dogs rate high on the Duchess's animal priorities, and here she gives her views on the respect due to the domestic dog in today's society.

To me, dogs are dogs and the mongrel deserves the same consideration as the thoroughbred. Until recently I always had labradors, two of which were strays, but my present four dogs are all small. Their ancestry is very mixed, but I detect some Pekinese cairn and even Tibetan spaniel. The two eldest are out of the same litter, by a peke out of a mixed-up cairn. One is dark and the other light in colour, and the little light one is always sitting up like a ferret and trying to talk. They go everywhere with me, and accompany me to all my meetings.

There is a big job to be done in combating the present appalling numbers of unwanted and homeless dogs. I was delighted when the National Canine Defence League decided to spay bitches before releasing them to new owners. This is a very practical and progressive move and I hope other organisations will follow their example.

Much is done for stray dogs by local sanctuaries all over the country, and my daughters and I started the Climping

Sanctuary near Arundel. However, efforts of this kind can only operate successfully if funds are forthcoming. We have inaugurated a League of Friends, so that people whose dogs already enjoy a happy family home can contribute towards the cost of maintaining those less fortunate. We promote membership by inviting subscribers to a 'dog party' in the grounds of Arundel Castle. The invitations are addressed to the dog, inviting him or her to bring their master or mistress, and the idea proves very popular. People are very cooperative, especially the Chief Constable of Sussex, who kindly allows us to have a display by police dogs each year. To raise money, we run a mile of pennies when the castle is open to the public, which makes two thousand pounds, and subscriptions from the Friends total three thousand pounds.

Dogs have so much to offer, especially to the lonely and the elderly. At our local hospice, St Barnabas, visits by dogs are encouraged and I take mine to meet the residents. In most cases homes will not allow people to take their own pets when they move in, and I can understand that looking after animals as well as elderly and sometimes infirm people would present a tremendous problem. However, for an elderly person to lose the privacy of their home and the companionship of their pet at the same time is a double blow, and visits by friendly owners with their dogs can be a considerable help. I understand that this idea is growing rapidly and I welcome the trend.

There is much to be gained by us all if we can give animals a good life and enjoy what they have to give in return.

42
THE BADGERS' TALE
An interview with Nigel Pierce

*For the past fourteen years Nigel Pierce and his wife Carol have
tended injured animals. Formerly the warden of a nature reserve,
Nigel now runs the Sheba Bird Sanctuary at St Leonards-on-
Sea, Sussex. Named in memory of Sheba, a much-loved Great
Dane, the registered sanctuary cares not only for birds, but for
many injured or abandoned animals which are brought in by
police, doctors, vets, local fishermen and members of the public.*

Honey, the badger cub, arrived one evening in the arms of a
local farmer. A few weeks earlier the same man had brought
us a guillemot, badly covered in oil, and had taken note that
we were accustomed also to treating badgers and foxes. This
farmer has no less than thirty setts on his land and he thinks
the world of his badgers.

Carrying the badly injured cub in his hat, he told us the
little badger had been savaged by one of his Jack Russell
terriers. His vet had given her an antibiotic and now he was
asking us if we could try to nurse her back to health for him.
The little cub was badly hurt and in a state of shock, and we
were doubtful whether she would survive the night. However,
we fed her every half-hour with a special milk and glucose
mixture, and the following morning she appeared to be coping
very well. We tried other nourishment and she soon showed
a liking for melted honeycomb. Thus she became Honey.

The next weekend the farmer called again, fully expecting
bad news, and was delighted to find Honey greatly improved.
All she needed was careful nursing and the company of her
own kind. And then a miracle happened. Two weeks after

Honey's arrival we received another badger cub, found on a site which was being developed. The sett had been disturbed, and she had clearly been wandering about for a number of days and was covered in ticks. We spent several hours getting rid of these and then took her to our vet. He said she was anaemic and put her on a course of multivitamins. She soon began to thrive on the same special diet as Honey and they enjoyed each other's company. We christened her Sugar.

When cubs are young, constant play is a natural feature of their development, and my wife and I became heavily involved. Too young and as yet not fit enough to survive outside, the cubs made a sett behind the settee in our sitting room, from which they would appear and invite us to play with them. This was most enjoyable, but very time-consuming! Recently, after many weeks of careful feeding and attention, they built themselves a sett outside in a spare aviary, where they now sleep most of the day and welcome a visit from us in the evenings.

Honey and Sugar will both go back to our farmer friend before long, and it is important that they should get used to the food they will find in the wild. So we have now to provide dead birds, rabbits, insects, snails, slugs, shrews and vegetables – an intimidating shopping list!

Looking after Honey and Sugar has been a joyful experience, despite the anxiety of the early days. We are more accustomed to treating adult badgers, mostly the result of road accidents. One has to be extremely cautious in handling them; in their pained and shocked condition, they will bite through the thickest gloves, and they can be as big and as strong as an average pig. A few years ago we took in a big badger which had been hit by a car. The vet had to wire his jaw and we had him in a cage for five months. I am happy to say he now has his own sett and a lady companion, and they live undisturbed in a wood on private land.

At any one time we will have thirty or forty birds in the sanctuary; our records show that last year we had a total of over eight hundred. Being by the sea, the majority of casualties are gulls and guillemots who have fallen foul of oil, sewage and other sea and beach pollution, such as plastic litter. Sewage produces bacteria which cause paralysis in seabirds, and this is a very common occurrence. Fortunately, the treatment is simple – five to six days of no food, just plain water, which flushes out the bird's system, after which it can be released again into the air.

Keeping the various species of guests properly separated is an important part of organising our kind of sanctuary. We often have to receive foxes, for instance, and indeed we took in a young cub soon after the arrival of Honey and Sugar. This little fellow was severely injured in the chest and had to be operated on by our vet. He is now convalescing well and running around, and is a source of infinite curiosity to our housedogs, whose attempts to play with him are received with timid caution. On the other hand, the dogs must be kept well away from the badger cubs, who are now big enough and strong enough to kill them if the opportunity arose.

As we buy sprats from the fishmonger to feed to our gulls, we never cease to wonder at nature's scheme of interdependence and our privilege to minister to so many different creatures.

43
BURMESE – THE
QUEEN'S HORSE
An interview with Robin Porter RVM

When Robin Porter was called up for his National Service, he chose to serve his term in the Military Police, with the object of joining the Metropolitan Police on demobilisation. After an initial three years in the Force, he applied and was accepted into the Mounted Branch.

Having recently retired after thirty years' service, Robin Porter tells of his good fortune in being chosen to take charge of Burmese. This led to the privilege of personally serving the Queen for ten eventful years and the award of the Royal Victorian Medal in 1987. The RVM is an honour in the personal gift of Her Majesty.

I always wanted to be a policeman, and after the customary probationary period on the beat, I applied for the Mounted Branch. A cockney born and bred, I knew nothing about horses, nor had I ever ridden one, but the decision I came to out of the blue turned out to be the best I have ever made.

My first posting was to the station in Hyde Park, where there is a police stable, and at that time Princess Margaret used to ride on Rotten Row. She had her own horse, Wangy, which was kept in the police stables in the care of one of the officers. When the officer became the first £40,000 winner of the football pools, he retired. His successor then had an operation and I was requested to take over. I took Wangy to the Royal Mews at Buckingham Palace when needed, and that was my introduction to the job of looking after horses for royalty. I became involved in training horses specifically for royal and senior army riders, including Prince Philip, Prince Charles and the Crown Equerry, Sir John Miller.

For a long time, horses for ceremonial purposes had been trained by the Metropolitan Police, each horse doing approximately a two-year tour of duty. However, in 1969 Burmese was presented to the Queen by the people of Canada, through the Royal Canadian Mounted Police, and that year she did her first royal parade. This resulted in a break with tradition. The Queen now had her own horse and she rode Burmese exclusively for the next eighteen years. Burmese came to her as a ready-trained parade horse, and the Rolls-Royce of animals for ceremonial purposes.

She is a petite horse, standing sixteen two hands, completely black with a lush coat that reminded her trainer in Canada of a Burmese cat, hence her name. She was the pride of the Canadian Mounted Police and on a state visit to Canada, the Queen, seeing her perform in a musical ride, recognised at once her regal qualities and picked her out.

For the first eight years of her life in England, Burmese was based at Windsor and throughout the year she was used as a hack by the Queen, riding in Windsor Great Park. Six weeks before the Trooping of the Colour she would come up to London to Great Scotland Yard police stables for a refresher course, getting her used to the streets, the crowds and riding in Hyde Park. During this period the Queen would continue to ride her, either in the Royal Mews or at Windsor.

The day after the Birthday Parade we would take about eight horses down to Windsor for Royal Ascot. These were police horses, to be available for the Queen's house guests to ride in the Great Park, and Burmese would also go. We would spend the week with the horses and also ride with the Queen. It was decided by Her Majesty that Burmese should be looked after by the Metropolitan Police on a full-time basis, on the understanding that she was available to the Queen whenever required.

In 1977 the Canadians presented the Queen with a second horse, Centennial. This was a nephew of Burmese and I was put in charge of him. However, when Burmese came back full-time to the police, the officer who had been looking after her on the occasions when Burmese was not at Windsor left to go to our training establishment at Imber Court, and I was asked to take over. That was how I came to look after Burmese.

There followed the ten most interesting and rewarding years of my life. When I took over Burmese, she was about fifteen years old and a bit of a tartar. If you have a spirited horse, you have to work it very hard and keep it down to work. If not, it will try to buck you, and will bolt and do all kinds of stupid things. But Burmese was a manageable horse, and once she got used to me she understood and accepted our relationship. She was a horse of exceptional character: a regal horse, a loner, and one whose natural place was out in front. Horses have a herding instinct and they tend to gather together, but Burmese would always be on her own, with her head in the air.

My most worrying time was always the day before the Trooping. Burmese is the most photographed and one of the most famous horses in the world, and when she went on parade with the Queen on her back, she had to be in absolutely pristine condition. I suppose that for eight out of my ten years with her this was so. However, on one occasion as I led her out of her box, somebody closed the door on her tail and left half of it hanging on the door. We quickly gathered up all the hair and stuck it back on with Superglue. Burmese, of course, was quite unaware of what had occurred, but as I turned the horse out for the day my heart was in my mouth, wondering if the mended tail would be noticed. To my great relief I was complimented on her superb turnout!

Another incident concerned the weather. Trooping always takes place at 11 a.m. on the second Saturday in June, or in the afternoon if the morning is wet. On two occasions in my thirty years of police service it had to be held on the Sunday. The year I have in mind, the procession started off out of the Palace gate and the heavens opened. The rain fell down in torrents, but having started they carried on. My duty, having seen the Queen mounted, was to jump into a car and go down to the Horseguards Parade and wait behind the gates in case I was required, and then be back in the Palace when they returned, to take over the horse again.

All this time I was under cover, and as the royal party returned up the Mall there was another cloudburst, while I waited under the arch inside the Palace. As the Queen approached me, she stopped and tipped her head forward, so that the water from her headgear gushed all over me. She looked at me with a smile and said: 'If I am going to get wet, you are going to get wet too.'

In the police force there were only a few people allowed to ride Burmese, and in the six weeks' run-up to Trooping time, when the Queen was riding daily, getting herself acclimatised to the side-saddle, then only I could ride the horse. On royal weddings and funerals, Burmese would take part in a purely police capacity. It could be controlling crowds outside Westminster Abbey or St Paul's, and after the Trooping we would do duty at demonstrations and football matches. She had no special treatment at all, and although some senior officers were a little concerned about this policy, I was given complete licence as to how the horse should be worked. I feel quite proud of that, being only a sergeant in a vast organisation like the Metropolitan Police.

I have given the impression that Burmese was a tartar, but that is part of the character of a good horse. I can honestly say that in all the years we worked together, among the crowds, the visitors, the demonstrators, she never gave me one moment's anxiety.

Burmese was retired from duty in 1986. She was twenty-four years old and the Queen decided that she should not be ridden again. Police horses usually retire at twenty – roughly the equivalent of a human retiring age of sixty – and, like humans, after that age various organs begin to deteriorate, but Burmese had four extra years of good service. I kept her for a further year and then she was put out to grass at Windsor. Now she has a paddock of her own in the park, right outside the Queen's own apartments, where she spends the day, returning to her stable at night. She has a couple of brood mares with her in the paddock to keep her company, but she remains regal and aloof.

I go down to see her from time to time. It is difficult to judge whether she remembers me; a horse is more likely to remember someone who has treated her badly. However, she comes over and nuzzles up, and we have a chat while I give her some sugar. I like to think she knows me and shares my happy memories of the wonderful years we served the Queen together.

44
HAPPY ENDINGS
by M. Raymonde-Hawkins MBE

There can be few, if any, people living today with longer exper-
ience of caring for animals than Miss M. Raymonde-Hawkins,
who began as a voluntary worker with the Cats Protection League
branch in Worthing over sixty-five years ago. A teacher by profes-
sion, she subsequently gave her services to Our Dumb Friends
League (now Blue Cross) and in 1955 opened her own animal
sanctuary, Raystede, in Sussex. Living always 'over the shop'
Miss Raymonde-Hawkins personally directs the policy and the
daily working of Raystede, which now extends over many acres
and is excellently equipped to house and care for many species.

The following stories and a final comment from her book Sensible Pets and Silly People *speak for themselves.*

THE OWLS

One of the most surprising and horrifying phone calls that
Raystede has ever had was from a man who said he wished
us to take two owls which he had kept apart but tied up for
fourteen months! He had bought them as babies in a pet
shop but now they were becoming vicious!! A not surprising
development for two creatures born for freedom, tied by their
legs from babyhood and given no water and suitable feed!

Our former greenhouse was immediately prepared for them
and they arrived, still tied by their legs, staring at each other
but unable to approach and about a yard apart. The owner
laid down various strict rules for us to obey:

They must never have water.
They must never be untied.
They must never get near each other as they would fight.

Our observation showed us that they were young, handsome, beautifully white and an obvious pair, so our veterinary surgeon untied the thongs that had so long imprisoned them, allowed them water and a bath and released them into our old greenhouse. Because they had never exercised their wings or their limbs, it was impossible to release them immediately into the wild but, far from attacking each other when released, they immediately flew to one another and remained for weeks always sitting side by side by day and making faltering flying efforts by night on to the spars of the roof. It was necessary to keep them confined until their wings had grown strong.

Their obvious devotion to each other developed and in the spring eggs appeared and She sat remotely in her box and He sat on guard outside while She carefully cared for, and successfully hatched out, two beautiful babies. They grew daily and within weeks we had difficulty in knowing babies from parents. Captivity for these youngsters was wrong and so they were in the fullness of time taken in a large cage up to the Queen Mother's Shelter, which overlooks our lakes and is surrounded by trees; there they were fed for a little while and then their cage was left open. For a time they stayed around and occasionally, years after, we hear them at nights, but happily they have gone off together to lead a natural life in the trees, where food from our warden is available.

Happily their life now will be unlike that of their unfortunate parents, whose early life has been so cruelly wrong. Even now the parents cannot be trusted to fly and have no idea of catching their own food or leading quite normal lives, and so they have the freedom of the grass space around the greenhouse. They have a nesting box (or rather a barrel) up in the tree and exercise their wings by night and feed regularly from food that is taken to them which is not too unnatural, although the method of receiving it, of course, gives them no opportunity to search for their own, which they have never learnt to do due to their early life of captivity.

PINKIE

Pinkie was one of a group of animals rescued a few years ago from unsatisfactory conditions in Vienna.

Six dogs, a cat and a monkey were owned by a circus proprietor. All had travelled Europe in uncomfortably small cages performing their 'acts' to countless audiences. At the point that we met them, their owner was ill and they were in the so-called 'care' of a shelter for animals, but two of the six dogs had died through fights, and the monkey who shared its crate with the stone-deaf cat had become fierce.

From these conditions we evacuated the six that remained and made it impossible for them ever again to suffer the agonising glare of footlights, or the misery of cramped travelling conditions.

We arranged to dispatch by air to England two of the dogs and the monkey (at this point they were not our property and had to be kept alive). Two of the dogs and the little cat found a delightful home with our friends in Switzerland.

Pinkie, the monkey, has developed into a nearly human four-footer with engaging ways that endear her to strangers but, although she has lost the memory of her misery days in the circus, she retains many of her habits, and spends hours in this upright position, but on a luxurious cushion and no longer haunted by the discipline of the sawdust ring.

SAM

We have almost accepted that puppies and kittens that have been given as Christmas presents get neglected and discarded by the new year, but less frequently, I hope, comes the story of such as Sam the pony.

Sam is now enjoying the company of donkeys in our President's Field behind the sanctuary.

Recently he made the journey down from London in the care of kind friends who had watched his deterioration over nearly two years since he was bought one Christmas as a present for a child who did not particularly want to love Sam, did not even really want to ride Sam, but did want to be able to say she had a pony of her own, the same as other girls at her school.

Sam was accordingly mounted by the child, who knew nothing of riding, and an accident ensued, damaging Sam's eye. From that moment, fear of riding and total lack of interest in the animal ensued, and he was left in a field with no shelter, no love, no education, and watched by friends who were concerned for his welfare, until they managed to possess him and bring him down to Raystede.

He was so happy at finding a field and companionship that he raised his head for the first time for a long while. He trotted and even seemed to grow bigger in the possession of his own stable, shelter, food, companionship and the joy of our fields.

*   *   *

The responsibility which is placed upon mankind as the controlling and intellectual animal demands that our relationships with the lesser animals, whether in so-called sport or other contacts, should be of such a calibre that the highest moral principles of our behaviour one to another will be reflected in our relationship to all forms of life.

Although my work as an animal welfarer has satisfied my reason for living by ameliorating the immediate suffering of animals, yet, in fact, predominantly my service must be that of a humanist. For while others depend on psychology and religion to educate mankind to the highest moral standards, my vocation has been, through animal welfaring, to aim at raising man's attitude to his fellows. Having accepted universal kinship, we must work in unity in the great brotherhood of life, for whatever its colour or creed, and whether it walks on two legs or on four, it demands full reverence, respect and justice.

45
FELINE FRIENDS
An interview with Beryl Reid OBE

From her first stage appearance at Bridlington as a young girl, Beryl Reid has enjoyed a non-stop career in the British theatre. The list of her West End plays is almost inexhaustable and her equal command of comedy, tragedy and pathos has ensured her a unique reputation.

Radio and television have both benefited from her personal series and in 1983 she won the BAFTA Award for best TV actress. Here she tells of her family of cats and how it all began.

It all started by accident, about forty years ago and soon after I had moved into the riverside cottage where I still live.

A wild cat had her kittens in the straw lagging around the water tank in the roof. I heard crying, and on going up to investigate I found these four little kittens. There was no mother to be seen at the time and I felt the right thing to do was to bring them down to be fed and looked after. However, the mother was in the vicinity, and because we had handled them she killed them – all except Footie. The most advanced of the kittens, she grew to be a long-haired black cat and lived to a grand old age of twenty. From my local RSPCA I obtained Fred, to be her companion as my work took me away frequently. Footie had an uncanny intuition, she was a kind of witch's cat who seemed to know everything. On one occasion I went away to Newquay for four days and my housekeeper told me that Footie disappeared immediately after I left and returned, four days later, shortly before I reached home.

With one or two exceptions, all my cats have come from my local RSPCA branch, whose people do the most wonderful work under very difficult conditions. They have been very good to me – and still are – and whenever I am offered a fee for a speaking engagement, I always ask for a small cheque for my RSPCA.

Today I have a family of ten cats. They are all individuals and each has a preference for the siting of their food saucer. One will favour a particular corner, another a windowsill, and they all feed from their own saucer. Cats are scrupulously clean and even fastidious about their food. This presents a medical problem when pills or tablets are prescribed. To administer medication to a dog is simple: you just mix it in with his food and he will gobble it up without being aware of it. But not cats! Everything in the saucer is meticulously inspected and anything suspect is left.

I once had a little cat called Georgie Girl and I managed to put an orange-coloured lozenge into her mouth each day, as prescribed by the vet. I thought I had done rather well until I discovered, one day, a tidy row of orange lozenges outside the back door on the mat.

One of my most unusual experiences concerns Elsie, whom I brought home from Bristol in 1979. I was playing at the Bristol Old Vic, in a play called *Born in the Gardens*, and I noticed this underfed young cat near to my flat. She always seemed afraid of something and would hide under cars and get herself covered with oil. I found out that she belonged to a family with three Indian children – the mother was a German radiologist married to a Sikh – and I knew the cat was ill-treated. So I used to put cat food down for her when I came home from the theatre. I wrote my name in red nail varnish on a saucer and I would place it behind the railings of the house. These people had a very strange way of life and I vividly remember that when I eventually managed to get into the house, there was very little furniture and bare floorboards, but an enormous television set and a big fridge freezer. I said to the woman, 'What do you call your cat?' After some hesitation she said, 'Pussy.' 'Oh,' I replied, 'that must have been difficult to decide upon.' From then on she was Elsie, a character from *Born in the Gardens* frequently referred to but who never appeared.

After some discussion – and protests by the children – it was agreed that I might take the cat, and she came home with me. That was only the beginning! When we reached home I took her into the spare room, in which the wardrobe had a mirror front. Elsie had evidently never seen a mirror and she spent hours spitting at herself. She was extremely frightened of people and even after three months she was still very wild. And then one day a miracle happened. I shouted to her, at the top of my voice: 'How would you like a one-way ticket to the vet, Elsie?' – and from that moment she changed completely. In a day she became a different cat, calm and relaxed, and since then I have always made a point of speaking to her quietly. Elsie must be getting on for twenty now and one thing about her has never changed. Whenever I cook curry, she goes all funny and retires into a corner. I suppose it still reminds her of her life in Bristol in the same way that memories of our youth always remain with us.

Dimly and Muriel are brother and sister. They are seven years old, and Dimly is known as the poseur. He likes to be king of the castle and is mischief personified. He once chased a fox cub up a drainpipe and on another occasion he fell off a willow branch into the river.

Dimly got his name in an unusual way. Some visiting friends of mine were looking for me and one of them, spotting me across the carport, said, 'There she is! I can just see her moving dimly.' As I had the cat in my arms, the name stuck.

But names can make complications. I once had a cat called Sir Harry, an enormous tabby, and in the evening I used to be heard calling out: 'Come along, Sir Harry, we're going to bed now!' Luckily, I have no neighbours. Twilight is quite an event here, when I call the cats in for the night. That is the time when we put out food for the hedgehogs and the foxes, for which they literally queue up.

None of my cats like fish, but cats in general are fascinated by the movement in the water. When I was filming *Entertaining Mr Sloane* at Camberwell Cemetery, the gravediggers gave me a little cat. She used to stand on the bottom step in the garden and catch fish with one paw. She didn't like them to eat – it was just the compulsion of the chase.

Cats help one to relax. People who live with them rarely have heart trouble or high blood pressure. I look in envy sometimes at the way cats behave and their quiet, elegant dignity. They stroll along like fashion models – and that, of course, explains the origin of the word 'catwalk'. They put down their feet, one after the other, carefully and deliberately.

You can never make cats do what you want them to do. People have come here to photograph me with the cats, and when they arrive there is not a cat to be seen. Roy Plomley came here once, when I was doing 'Favourite Things', and he had a man here for three days, with an Arriflex camera on his shoulder, just photographing cats. They became so used to him that they would come and play with him. Shock treatment does not work – you have to give them time. On the other hand, they are very easy to train, especially if you have them as kittens. You only have to scratch in the litter tray with your fingers and they know instinctively that the tray is their loo. They are very bright.

I am appalled at the cruelty meted out to animals in this country, where we have a reputation as animal lovers. I have two cats, Billy and Clive, who, as kittens, lived in a dog kennel and people threw stones at them. Even now they are nervous of strangers. Elsie, when she lived in Bristol, used to be swung around by the tail, and many of my cats have come to me showing evidence of maltreatment.

Today I have ten cats. Tomorrow it could be eleven. It would take a book to describe them all, with their individual little ways, but I can recommend the stray cat as a loyal and worthwhile companion.

46

ANIMALS AND THE CHILD

by The Hon. Miriam Rothschild CBE FRS

Miriam Rothschild is the daughter of the late Hon. Charles Roths-child and, like her father, is an eminent biologist and entomologist. She has many academic honours and has published about three hundred scientific papers..

In the following extracts from her book Animals and Man, *Dr Rothschild reflects on her attitude towards animals as a child and her growing awareness of the respect due to them.*

As a child I owned a tough fox terrier called Nelly, who slept under my bed. Like so many of her breed she found moving objects irresistible – chasing and killing my grandfather's pinioned ornamental pheasants, as well as streaking after motor vehicles. My mother, who knew how deeply I loved Nelly, concealed her depredations from my grandfather, but one fine day the little dog was killed chasing a motor-cycle down Tring High Street. The nursemaid bustled me along so that I never saw Nelly lying in the road but I still recall my deeply shocked disbelief. Surely Nelly's twinkling paws could never stop moving? 'Shall I meet Nelly again in Heaven?' I asked the nursemaid, in an agonised whisper. 'No', replied the girl authoritatively: 'Dogs are animals – they don't go to Heaven.'

It never occurred to me to ask her how she knew. I accepted what grown-ups said as if they were in direct communication with the Almighty, but from that moment onwards I became secretly highly critical of God. If dogs were not admitted, I had little use for Heaven either. Curiously enough, although I chattered freely and incessantly with my parents about the events of the day, I never discussed these feelings, which seemed to belong to something apart.

A replacement, 'Susie', was duly found for poor Nelly. Looking back, I fancy my dogs were considerably more important to me than my siblings. I never felt an urge to photograph my brother or sisters and certainly I never dreamed of writing their tedious lifestories, whereas I planned to immortalise Susie with an illustrated biography and spent all my pocket money on films for that purpose. Susie was uncooperative. (I have never yet owned a dog which liked being photographed. At the sight of the camera one and all would slink away, and if obedient to a command to sit still, lashed back their ears and assumed an expression of acute misery.)

Nor did I worry much when my sisters were punished, bumped their heads, or went down with influenza, but I minded acutely if my dogs were scolded or sick. Furthermore I never planned to give my brother or sisters their favourite chocolates or sweets, nor a 'good time', whereas I regularly sneaked titbits for Susie and, to please her, took her rabbiting every afternoon. Susie was a desperately keen but inept hunter, but one day she actually appeared carrying a moribund baby rabbit. It was still warm, but, at this age, I felt no compassion, only immense satisfaction on her behalf. I lavished praise upon her: 'Good Susie, clever, *clever* Susie!' She looked smug. At last I got a snapshot – a bit out of focus due to the excitement of the unbelievable happening. For me camaraderie and larks and rivalry and demon patience were shared enthusiastically with the siblings; but solicitude, affection, and caring were reserved for Susie.

As far as I was concerned the long line of dogs which followed Susie down to the present day each taught me something. 'Anyone who has kept a horse or a dog [wrote Alister Hardy] and got really fond of them can't doubt that they are conscious beings like ourselves.'

In the western world we are rather uncaring for the old members of the community – unlike the Chinese – but we have one saving grace which makes up for our multiple sins of omission: we have selectively bred dogs which are fond of us, young and old people alike.

Looking back I realise that a dog or a cat in the home is the most powerful tool there is for teaching children how to behave, how to care, and the meaning of goodwill. Unfortunately few even affluent parents seize this opportunity, nor do they give serious thought to the requirements of their pets. It is customary to see children dragging a dog along, mercilessly, by a collar and lead, without eliciting a word of reproof or explanation from their adult companions.

Perhaps it is a little far-fetched to consider fur coats under the heading of animals in the home but this is relevant to the upbringing of children. I need hardly say that in my personal view the fur trade should be phased out, and successful actresses should find a better way of advertising their Oscars. In this part of home life we have one singularly cheering precedent. Before World War I, two or three hundred million tropical birds were killed annually to supply the millinery trade. Not only is the importing of foreign bird feathers now illegal, but no women would contemplate appearing in a hat decorated with birds of paradise plumes. Doubtless in time – one hopes soon – fur coats will suffer the same fate as feather hats, especially since synthetic substitutes are now available. It will be a good moment when a parent can say to a child, 'Believe it or not, people used to wear fur coats – yes, baby seal coats – and put humming bird feathers in their hats. . . .'

* * *

I loved horses and riding. Both proved exhilarating. I soon discovered you could see more of the countryside, and experience the thrill of getting quite close to the wildlife of the woods and fields, from the back of a pony than on two feet. Curiously enough the knowledge I gained in this way gave me a sense of superiority over the folk who walked or drove along roads and well-worn paths. One day a neighbour's daughter, whom I rather admired, suggested I got permission to go 'cubbing' with her. Thereafter I hunted with the local pack of foxhounds twice a week. First and foremost it was an escape from a nagging governess and solitary, insufferably boring lessons; secondly it was a whole day's riding in the company of a group of jolly contemporaries; thirdly it was both interesting and very exciting. I firmly believed what I was told, namely, that only fox-hunting preserved The Fox. Otherwise, like the wolves in England, this lovely animal would have long been exterminated. Now, for each fox hunted and perhaps caught and killed, a score lived happily in the woods. My first uneasy moments occurred when the late John Fryer indicated that one could not, unfortunately, ask foxes for their views, which, indeed, might be very different from my own. Then one day I was waiting with a group of riders while the hounds were noisily drawing a small cover alongside us. Suddenly a slim red fox emerged from the bushes, ran for a few yards into the field, stopped to urinate and then fled on towards a distant hedgerow. It looked very small and frightened. One of the women riders laughed loudly. '*Do* you see *that?*' she cried. 'It's actually sitting down!'

I suddenly realised, with a prickly feeling beneath my scalp, that this pastime was extremely cruel. I gave up hunting.

47

THE CHURCH COULD DO BETTER

An interview with The Bishop of Salisbury

Educated at Oriel College, Oxford, and Cuddesdon Theological College, the Rt Rev. John Baker had a distinguished career as lecturer in theology and Hebrew in various Oxford colleges between 1959 and 1973, when he became Canon of Westminster. From 1978 to 1982 he was Sub-Dean, Rector of St Margaret's, Westminster, and Chaplain to the Speaker of the House of Commons.

Since 1982, as Bishop of Salisbury, he has attained a reputation for his outspoken views on the subject of animal welfare and for his criticism of the attitude of the Church of England. He says, 'Three major interests in addition to my regular ministry have been Northern Ireland, nuclear warfare and animal welfare, and I have been accused of masochism in taking on all three!'

I am very sorry that the Church in general is a little chary of the subject of animal welfare. We hear the usual excuses about the priority of concern for starving or ill-treated human beings, but if you feel compassion for one living creature, then you surely feel it for another – and if you feel compassion for a human being, how can you stifle it for an animal?

I suspect that part of the trouble with the Church of England is its respectability. The Church prefers not to be associated with people who are thought to be a little odd or cranky or overenthusiastic. Pictures of animal rights campaigners do not match up with good, solid Church of England dignity.

Moreover, in the country areas people who are pillars of

the congregation can often be involved in activities of which the animal welfare movement is critical. Some time ago I went to a Harvest Thanksgiving and Supper in a parish where one of the churchwardens was a Master of Foxhounds and the other kept a battery hen unit. The vicar was rather scared that the occasion might develop into a riot, and indeed one of the bellringers, before the service began, warned me, 'Now, don't you be too hard on us farmers!' In fact, the evening was a happy one. All concerned were very kind, and I tried to pursue my normal policy of presenting a balanced view in my sermon. Food has to be produced; farmers have to make a proper living; and animals have to be treated with respect. I believe our responsibility is to employ the superior brain we have been given to devise ways of satisfying the needs of all – humans and animals alike – and I would like to see more effort put into finding solutions.

Among the wider issues of our relationship with animals, the ones which have concerned me most are the questions surrounding farm animals – a very hot potato indeed. The slaughtering of animals, modern intensive methods of egg and chicken-meat production, the long-distance transportation of animals – all these are matters of major concern to me and they need much more attention.

By and large, our attitude towards animals is rooted in tradition. We eat them because we have always eaten them, and to become vegetarian involves a big break and a basic readjustment to new ways of shopping, cooking and eating. So it would appear that a major change in our relationship with animals is a matter for education. Most children, unless maladjusted, wish to be kind to animals. When very young, they may throw a puppy that bites to the floor, but that is before they have developed any sense of responsibility to others or realised that they are causing pain. Once they have grown to understand, they want to exercise responsibility. I believe that if animal relationships became part of the education curriculum, attitudes would gradually change for the better.

In my own case, my awakening occurred when our family

dog was left in kennels when we went on holiday. He caught distemper and died in our absence, and I felt this very keenly; but my reverence for animals did not emerge until some years later. I was given an air gun – a normal present for a growing boy in those days – and was encouraged to go and shoot grey squirrels, which were, and still are, regarded as destructive vermin. I shot my first squirrel – and my last. Having taken that life, I was overcome with horror at what I had done and was never able to contemplate shooting a squirrel or anything else again.

I realise there are many circumstances in which an animal must be destroyed – companion animals having to be put down through illness, and controlled culling to preserve the balance of nature – but I have never been able to understand how people can breed birds in order to kill them, or hunt foxes for enjoyment. Take, for instance, the situation in the New Forest, which is abundantly stocked with wild deer. The Forestry Commission carries out an annual cull, carefully planned and controlled, and this keeps down the population to an acceptable level. Parallel with this, the local buckhound hunt creates what seems to many of us quite unacceptable and cruel harassment of the herds in the name of sport, while killing only a relatively small number. What concerns me is that it seems impossible to get sensible dialogue between opposing interests to find better ways of doing whatever really needs to be done.

There is no need – and certainly no excuse – to treat animals unkindly. Wise farmers, from biblical times, have always recognised the value of well-treated cattle or beasts of burden, and for the great majority of us today the domestic pet, our only animal contact, is regarded with respect and affection. Some time ago my wife and I gave a home to an unwanted dog. Perhaps not the most intelligent of animals, Sammy is reasonably bright and very good company. His origin is questionable, but we describe him as a 'borderline collie' and, to us, he is another member of the family – or pack!

48
SON OF TIGER BAY
An interview with Colin Shepherd MP

Educated at Oundle and McGill University, Montreal, Colin Shepherd served in the Royal Canadian Navy before returning home to join Haigh Engineering Company as Marketing Director. In 1974 he was elected Member of Parliament for Hereford, which he still represents.

A Fellow of the Industry and Parliament Trust, Colin Shepherd is Chairman of the Library Sub-Committee and a member of other parliamentary committees. He is also Chairman of the All Party FRAME Parliamentary Group. He is married and has three children.

It all began in 1982, when some new people took over the farm next door, bringing with them a savage and malicious tomcat called Tiger Bay. This creature had a killer instinct, which soon became apparent when he set about carving out a territory for himself. The hotel across the road in our small hamlet had been adopted by an elderly cat who lived a quiet and blameless life, doing nobody any harm. However, there was a border clash and Tiger Bay killed it quite mercilessly.

The new incumbent had a common-law wife, who soon produced a litter of kittens. The whole family would be fed from the farmyard door every evening at six o'clock and this would proceed in true pecking order. Tiger Bay would first eat his fill, followed by Mrs Tiger Bay and then the kittens in order of aggressiveness. At the end of the queue was a small black runt who hardly got any food at all.

This kitten, despite his physical shortcomings, had a brain. He soon decided that there must be other places where food could be obtained, and took to presenting himself at our back doorstep. At this time the children were at school, I was commuting to Westminster and we had recently lost our family dog, which, having taken to chasing sheep, had had to be put down, much to our sorrow. We had therefore decided, as a matter of policy, not to have any further family pets of any kind for the foreseeable future.

Faced with the little bundle at our back door, we bravely stood firm in our determination not to be taken over, but we relented to the extent of putting out a little milk. Encouraged by this, of course, the kitten became a regular supplicant and the milk offering a regular daily drill. The kitten grew stronger, gained in confidence and then disappeared.

Ten days later I was out on an adjoining piece of land, where I have a garage, and as I approached I noticed a black tail sticking out from under the garage door and moving to and fro. This belonged to the missing kitten, who had evidently found his way into the garage and was unable to get out. Instead of mewing, he had backed up against the door when he heard someone approaching and waved his tail to attract attention. I was impressed, so I rescued him and gave him milk, and off he went a second time.

Eventually he began to adopt us, as it were. He increased the frequency of his visits and demands but remained quite independent – and so did we. He then took to exploring the kitchen and finally decided to lay claim to a selected spot in front of the Aga cooker, where it is always warm.

Tiger Bay was still in the district and tales of his misdemeanours reached us from time to time, and it occurred to us that by nurturing our own feline visitor, he would one day become strong enough to take on his father and put him in his place. This, in the course of time, evidently happened, because Tiger Bay has disappeared from the locality and 'son of' confidently patrols his territory.

The cat, I have to confess, is now an integral part of the household, but still on the same basis of visitor. He looks after himself in general terms, and there may well be other houses in which he is fed. We do not enquire. He comes and goes as he pleases, but if he is still *in situ* in front of the Aga at bedtime, he is politely shown the door. The initial invitation is always ignored – he pretends to be deaf – but he eventually concedes and departs into the night.

One strange thing defies explanation. No matter what time of day we may return home – and we may have been away for several hours or several days – by the time the car has stopped and the front door is opened, the cat is sitting in the drive, watching us. I am always reminded of the Cheshire Cat, who would suddenly materialise without warning.

Although we still accept no responsibility for the cat (he does not even have a name) there are occasions when steps have to be taken in his own interests. One such was when we noticed that the Aga-hugging creature was visibly suffering from worms. It was a Sunday and the vet was unobtainable. However, some neighbours who keep Alsatians had some worm pills designed for their dogs, and there was no alternative but to borrow these and hope for the best. They were duly administered that evening, the cat was turned out – and we did not see him again for two weeks! When he did reappear, he was fitter, sleeker and in absolutely top form.

I suppose we have, in a way, spoiled the cat, which is now a confirmed milkaholic. He will employ any device to persuade visitors to give him milk, especially when my wife and I are not in the room. His tactics involve three stages. Stage One is rubbing affectionately against legs. Stage Two involves climbing up trousers and Stage Three, in desperation, consists of embedding painful claws into human flesh, accompanied by the pathetic cries of a starving cat. On the whole, visitors succumb in the early stages, but the exercise can be quite embarrassing.

One area where there is open warfare concerns our house martins. These charming but impudent birds like teasing the cat by divebombing him as he sits outside – mostly with impunity, as they do so with considerable speed. The cat pretends not to know, until he suddenly makes a leap and takes one on the wing. We are fond of our house martins and do our best to discourage this game. Some time ago the cat had just got his bird and came trotting across the lawn. I cornered him and forced him to relinquish the bird, which appeared unharmed and flew into a small hidey-hole in the side of the house. I kept the cat locked in the kitchen for half an hour and talked to him quite severely, but on being released, he made straight for the bird's hide, which by then was deserted. I shall never forget his look of disgust.

I have always been led to believe that whilst a family can own a dog, one cannot own a cat. We have never wished to do so, as I have been at pains to explain, but I am rapidly coming to the conclusion that, contrary to our wishes, the son of Tiger Bay thinks he owns us – and he may well be right.

49
WE DON'T OWN THE WORLD
An interview with David Shepherd OBE FRSA

Born in 1931 and educated at Stowe, David Shepherd started his career as an aviation artist and was a founder member of the Association of Aviation Artists. In 1960 he began painting African wildlife and held his first one-man show in London in 1962, a second in 1965 and exhibited in Johannesburg in 1966 and 1969. He has also painted portraits of HM the Queen Mother (for The King's Regiment), HE Dr Kenneth Kaunda, President of Zambia, and HE Sheikh Zaid of Abu Dhabi.

In the USA in 1971 he raised sufficient funds from the auction of his paintings to purchase a helicopter to combat game-poaching in Zambia and two years later raised a further £127,500 for Operation Tiger with his painting Tiger Fire. *In 1979 he was made a Member of Honour of the World Wildlife Fund, and was awarded the Order of the Golden Ark by HRH Prince Bernhard in 1973, the Order of the British Empire in 1980 and was elected a Fellow of the Royal Society of Arts in 1986.*

I became a wildlife artist quite by chance. I began as an aviation artist and in the course of my work I did many commissions for the RAF. In 1960 they invited me to fly to Kenya as their guest, there being at that time an RAF station at Nairobi. The officers there said they would like a couple of pictures for the mess, but not aeroplanes – 'we fly those all day; do you paint local things such as elephants?' 'No, but I'll have a go.' For that first picture I charged them twenty-five pounds. They've lost it, apparently; they're feverishly searching for it, as it might now be worth a little more! That chance commission changed my life overnight.

If there is one painting which established me as a wildlife artist, it is *Wise Old Elephant*. I painted it in 1962, but the publishers warned me that it would not sell. How wrong they turned out to be. That picture has since been reproduced in no less than a quarter of a million copies and is still selling. It is known affectionately as my 'elephant in Boots', as it appeared in every branch of Boots the Chemist.

Another experience during that visit to Kenya in 1960 made a profound impression on me and resulted in my becoming a dedicated conservationist. I saw two hundred and fifty-five dead zebra lying around a water hole. The water had been deliberately poisoned by poachers, in order to get the zebra skins. When I saw that sight, at the same moment as my career was taking off due to the wildlife I was painting, I naturally wanted to do something for wildlife in return. Since then, as I have learnt and seen what man is doing, the motivation has become stronger and more urgent every day. From that day the cause of wildlife conservation has been my priority in life.

In 1973 the World Wildlife Fund found there were only 1,837 Bengal tigers left in the whole of India. They were on the brink of extinction, as the black rhino is today. So the Fund set up 'Operation Tiger' and asked me to paint a picture to assist the appeal. I had never painted a tiger before, so off I went to India to see one. I failed, because they had mostly been shot or poisoned, to be turned into hearth rugs for human financial gain. However, John Aspinall came to the rescue. He has the largest collection of tigers in the world – around forty – and when I told him I wanted to paint a dramatic picture of a tiger and needed to photograph an angry one, he invited me down to his zoo in Kent.

John explained that all his tigers were so nice and friendly, it would be difficult to make one angry. However, he ushered me into the enclosure to meet Zarif, a large Siberian tiger. As this enormous creature came pounding towards me, I noticed that John had remained outside, and when the tiger skidded to a halt in a cloud of dust, I didn't really know what to do! To my relief he merely rubbed his head against my leg, just

like a domestic cat, then rolled over and went to sleep with
his legs in the air, smiling all over his face. I rubbed his
tummy and he started to purr. So far, the exercise had all the
promise of a total disaster.

The next step was quite unexpected. Zarif got up, lifted his
tail and urinated all over me. John was delighted, as this,
he said, showed the animal liked and accepted me! Having
established this rapport, the problem of making him angry
loomed again. John then had an idea. He informed me that
Zarif had not been fed for a week (information I was glad not
to have received when I first entered the enclosure). He would
give him a great hunk of beef and let him have ten minutes
to settle into it while I got in very close and focused on his
whiskers. Then, on a countdown, John would pull the meat
away and this should produce a very dramatic close-up of an
angry tiger.

The moment came, the lunch was pulled away – and Zarif
just smiled! Stepping on his foot was no better, but we finally
got a snarl by prodding him with a broomstick, which I hated.
The resulting photograph was the basis of the now well-known
Tiger Fire, which took me eight days to paint. We ran off 850
copies, which were sold at £150 each and raised £127,500 for
the campaign (one print had a lucky number, and the winner
received the original, free; that helped sell the prints!).

I now go to Africa about six times a year and the game
wardens take my wife and me out in their private Land
Rovers, so we are able to see much more than the tourists
can. I remember one occasion when we went out with Myles
Turner, the head game warden in the Serengeti. He was a
wonderful man, sadly no longer with us. It had been pouring
with rain and his windscreen wipers were going like the
clappers to try and keep the mud off the windscreen, without
much success. We stopped under a tree and a couple of chee-
tahs jumped on the bonnet, because they liked being above
ground level to get a good view. Myles Turner pushed down
his window, leaned out, got hold of a cheetah's tail and wiped
the windscreen with it! The cheetah took no notice at all; in
fact, I don't think he knew.

The stories of tourists told by the game wardens are legion and often scarcely credible. For instance, a busload of tourists 'doing' an African game park – they only had one afternoon as it was Japan next stop – were all armed with a list of the animals they could expect to see. An elephant was pointed out about three miles away and they all piled out of the bus, took a quick look, and ticked off 'elephant' on their list.

Then there was the American lady in the Tsavo National Park in Kenya – a lovely sub-tropical park and very hot – and she went up to the warden and asked, 'Do you get polar bears here?' With a face as straight as a poker he replied, 'Well, we do, madam, but the weather just now is very hot and they have gone up into the hills to get cool.'

The same warden, Tuffy Marshall – a great friend of mine – told me how he saw two nuns in full habit, sitting up a tree, without any vehicle in sight, while a rhino was standing beneath the tree, waiting for them to come down. It turned out that there were three nuns, but one had gone off in the vehicle temporarily while the other two sat in the tree to take photographs and await her return. Little did the two realise that they were to get some excellent close-ups of a rhino!

In some of the game parks in Africa there are animals which have become too accustomed to humans. They are not, of course, really tame, and frequently somebody oversteps the mark and frightens them; then there is the possibility of an accident. When that happens, it usually ends in the animal being shot.

John Clarke, the one-time head of the game department in Zambia, took an American visitor into the restaurant in one of the parks and they were sitting by the open window, having lunch. Suddenly the trunk of an elephant came through the window and started very gently going in between all the cruets, wine glasses, bottles, etc., on the table, carefully avoiding them all. John took no notice, it being a normal daily occurrence, but he looked up and saw his guest, his fork halfway to his mouth, paralysed with amazement. So, to ease the tension, he simply took hold of the trunk, coiled it up as one would a rope and pushed it out through the window.

Some of these animals are great characters. In Uganda, an elephant called the Lord Mayor used to stop everybody entering the park because he had become accustomed to people giving him fruit. This is where the danger starts, because the animal gets familiar, the visitor takes liberties and the accidents happen, through no fault of the animal. The Lord Mayor one day stopped a Volkswagen Beetle car which was crammed with Indians. He probably thought it was a large paper bag, so he put his trunk round it, lifted it and shook it. There is a photograph of it in one of my books, showing the car with just one wheel on the ground, while the elephant is shaking it in hope that the bananas will fall out. He did nobody any harm but finally I heard he had been shot. It was inevitable, but sad and very unfair.

Man is arrogant and foolish in his treatment of the world's resources. We don't own the world to do with it as we please – we share it with all living creatures, and we all depend on each other. Humans are the only animals that blow each other up with car bombs, engage in civil and international wars against our own species and destroy our environment through greed and ignorance, cutting down our forests and creating deserts.

This is the only world we have. We cannot make it any bigger, however clever we think we are; and it's high time that we started to treat it with some respect. I want my great-grandchildren, when I have them, to see elephants in their wild and natural state. (The elephant could be gone from the wild in thirty years.) Conservation is more important, even, than that; if we destroy everything around us, we finally go too. Of that there can be no doubt.

50
WALTER THE WARTHOG
by David Taylor

*David Taylor is a Fellow of the Royal College of Veterinary
Surgeons and of the Zoological Society of London. Originally a
vet in general practice, he decided some years ago to change direction and to concentrate on the wild and exotic species. His experiences as a freelance consultant to zoos and wildlife parks all over
the world have resulted in many books, and his television series
'One by One', which have delighted millions of readers and
viewers. His knowledge of even the less spectacular wild animals
provides many a good story, and in the following extract from his
book* Next Panda Please *he recalls a social encounter with a
warthog.*

'Do you like warthogs?' my hostess asked, as casually as other
folk might ask about one's taste in music or how many sugars
you take in your tea.

Up to that point I don't think I'd considered at any length
whether I was pro- or anti-warthog. I'd once smashed up a
car in northern Kenya by driving into a hole dug by a warthog:
they have a habit of building such pitfalls. On the other hand,
warthogs in zoos are generally very popular, affable creatures
that adapt well and have gentle natures. Their comical faces
attract the visitors and they give little trouble, being robust,
easy to feed and long-lived. On the few occasions that I'd had
to treat a warthog it had usually been for arthriticky joints
brought on by advancing years. One dear old soul at Belle
Vue Zoo, Manchester, had lived for sixteen and a half years
without a day's illness. Yes, very definitely, now that I came
to think about it, I liked warthogs a lot. I have found them,

like all members of the pig family, to be clean in their habits, intelligent and full of character.

'Yes,' I replied to the question, 'I like warthogs. Why?'

'There's a lovely warthog boar living in the bush not far away. Walter's his name. He absolutely adores potatoes. I'll go and fetch some and then we'll call him.'

My hostess was Betty Leslie-Melville, a remarkable lady who at her home in Kenya had raised a young giraffe, Daisy Rothschild, and returned her to the wild. Tame giraffes and now spuds as bait for a wild warthog! Betty Leslie-Melville certainly had a way with wildlife.

When she returned with a bag of potatoes, she told me to sit on the grass at the edge of the terrace with a small mound of the vegetables close to my feet. I was not to move or say anything. 'Walter is a bit on the nervous side,' she explained. Then she began calling towards the forest: 'Wal-ter! W-a-a-alter! Wa-a-a-a-alter!'

It was really rather exciting, sitting on the grass and waiting for the bush to yield up two hundredweights of untamed warthog with ferocious-looking curved tusks that may be over two feet in length. Tame as they may be in captivity, wild warthog boars can be dangerous, cantankerous individuals.

'Wa-a-a-a-lter!' Betty continued to call. 'He may perhaps be out of earshot, foraging with his band.'

Suddenly there was a warthog in the distance. Out of the woodland beyond the lawn he came, ears pricked and piggy tail curved high. He hesitated for a moment as he broke cover, stared in our direction and then began to trot towards us. Betty called his name one last time and then reminded me to stay still and silent.

Walter came on steadily. He was a magnificent individual, standing over two feet high with a pair of beady black eyes set in the knobbly, ferocious-looking face. His bristly head and bold and jaunty bearing reminded me strongly of a mou-stachioed and irascible sergeant-major. When he was ten yards from me the warthog stopped and eyed me intently. His tail was now held high in the air and the crest of straggly hair running down his back was partially raised. He sniffed, switched his gaze to the mound of potatoes and decided to risk a brush with the stranger. Ever so slowly he edged forwards, eyes darting up and down from me to the potatoes and back again. I could smell warthog now and I could see the cracks in the beauty mask of dried mud that covered his fierce face. I held my breath. It was a magical moment. No crush-cage, no tranquillisers, no ropes or bars or protective moats filled with water. Here was one of those rare occasions when, without the help of such artificial devices, one can meet a wild animal face to face. OK, so Walter was only a 'cupboard-love', out to freeload on the tasty potatoes, but even so, man as a rule is shunned by his fellow creatures as a dangerous and untrustworthy species, and exceptions to the rule are very precious.

Walter arrived at my shoes. He was wary and wound-up like a coiled spring. He gobbled tensely at the potatoes, his front feet doing a sort of little teetering dance, so anxious were they to get him away from the strange-smelling ape as soon as his meal was finished. Very, very slowly I moved my right hand down my legs. Walter kept his eye on me but continued to eat. My hand was twelve inches, then six, then three away from his curly upper tusks. Breathlessly I pushed my hand forwards just a fraction more. I touched the hard ivory. Walter finished his meal, grunted quietly and backed off, but I had actually touched a wild, conscious warthog. As Walter wandered aimlessly back towards the forest, his portly belly replete and his tail switching back and forth, I knew that this was the high point of my visit to Kenya.

51
RUNNING AROUND
IN CIRCLES
by F. J. Taylor Page MBE BSC

Jim Taylor Page was a schoolmaster in Norfolk and in Sussex before moving to Cumbria to found a field-studies centre for the Lowther Estate, in Askham, near Penrith. He is a Vice-President of both the Norfolk Naturalists Society and the British Deer Society.

He is a knowledgeable and entertaining local historian and national historian and his observations on the habits of the roe deer make fascinating reading. Among the generations of young people to whom Jim Taylor Page communicated his love of living creatures of all kinds was the Chairman of the FRAME Trustees.

Particularly in late July and early August, but sometimes earlier and occasionally in October, worn paths, often in the form of circles or figures of eight, may be discovered on the floor of clearances in open woodland or forest scrub – the natural habitat of the roe deer, the smallest of the indigenous species of their kind in Britain. Observation of how these roe deer rings originated has afforded me a lifelong fascination, though to this day, forty years from the time when I made my earliest notes and photographs, I can only hazard a guess at the real reason why these delightful animals have this unusual habit of running for long periods on circular tracks. Little has been written about them, probably because their activity is a nocturnal or early morning one, so it has rarely been observed and few have realised the significance of these runways, worn down to the bare soil by persistent use, though the evidence of the prints of small cloven hoofs is often to be found. They are quickly lost in the existent vegetation or by weathering, and frequently they must have gone unnoticed. Only from a strategically placed hide overlooking the forest arena can an observer appreciate what causes them.

Pursuit in a circle seems to be inherent in the existence of the roe. The twin fawns are trained by the doe, which spends considerable time in May and June chasing them and teaching them to double and twist – skills needed for safety in adult life. The choice of site is always very secluded and the play rings produced are large. I found one round a mound of soil excavated from a chalk pit, the ring almost brilliantly white and having a diameter of twenty feet. At other times the rings are smaller and less worn. Towards the beginning of July the doe is more preoccupied with mating activity and the fawns are left to look after themselves.

At the time of the rut, roughly between mid-July and early August, the buck pursues the doe, rousing her up with his nose and driving her ahead of him relentlessly, his nose as close to her tail end as can be maintained. Often she outstrips him and he breaks away, panting and exhausted. During the first week in August the pursuit may continue without pause through the night on to dawn and the early morning hours. Repeatedly the doe makes a high-pitched piping note. This is the call she uses to attract a buck; he can detect it at a considerable distance. I can imitate it with a special little whistle when I am in a hide, and, as if by magic, within a few minutes the buck in that territory will come in very close, seeking a mate.

It was while in just such a hide that I was able to watch the first stages in the formation of the rutting rings. As the doe breasted through the grass between the trees in a young plantation, she steered a winding course from left to right as if attempting to avoid the close attention of a buck hard pressing at her rear. These she encircled, always in an anticlockwise direction. Later I measured a few of these circles; their diameter was between three and four feet.

In making them, the doe needed no encouragement from the buck. Her winding course was deliberately chosen. The buck followed her every move. When she did break from one ring she occasionally encircled another object, but always she returned to her original circle anticlockwise, in this way creating a figure-of-eight course. Sometimes she would make off in long bounds, endeavouring to avoid pursuit. Sometimes she would lie down and the buck would thresh a small bush or tree, seemingly in frustration at being thwarted in his purpose of mating. Progressively the relentless chase slowed down, the circles diminished in size and activity resolved into a very close nose-to-tail encounter, the apparent purpose of the extraordinary behaviour, for ultimately the doe stood quietly while the buck covered her for a short period.

Such ring-making as a form of sex play is not unusual in animals other than roe deer. The ring is a form of display where the rhythms of male and female become synchronised. Naturalists have described analogous behaviour in African bush antelopes, the rose-coloured starling, Jackson's Whydah bird, hares and goats, and even a small type of spider. Moths of the genus Crambus circle in a ring about twelve inches in diameter.

But any form of animal progression seems to take the form of ritualised anticlockwise circling, from circus animals to greyhound racing. A Cambridge professor sent me details of the pursuit of two hedgehogs in the college garden, and observations of many different animals in movement on TV confirmed my general belief. Human beings do not escape! Just watch an athletics meeting, a roller-skating rink or a dance hall. We shake hands right-handed, except for the two per cent of us who are left-handed.

So is there something inherent in our make-up that determines this predilection? I can only think of the DNA helix, which is a left-handed spiral and the fundamental component of animals' muscle. So far as I know, no one has specifically examined the DNA of a left-handed person. I wonder if the spiral there is right-handed, i.e. governing clockwise instead of anticlockwise activity!

Perhaps a qualification is necessary relating to man's locomotory behaviour. It was expressed for me by a friend:

An epilogue is needed to say a few words
On poor Taylor Page, who lies dead–
The gyratory habits of mammals and birds
In the end quite affected his head.
Inscribed 'Here lies F.J.T., 92 years of age
In a small Lakeland churchyard his rock lies–
But all I've found out is he came to a roundabout
And just HAD to go round anticlockwise.'

52
VICTORY WITHOUT VIOLENCE
An interview with Angela Walder

One of the best-known activists in the animal welfare movement, Angela Walder has spent her life defending the treatment of animals and seeking to improve the lot of those mistreated by society. Not one to pull her punches and the scourge of all who fail to respect the dignity of animals, she has never advocated the use of violence, which she maintains is both immoral and counterproductive.

In 1987, appalled at the state of many catteries around the country, Angela Walder opened her own, the Arcadia Cat Hotel, in Minster on the Isle of Sheppey, where she lives.

The chief cause of my frustration with society is the mistreatment of animals and throughout my life I have done my very best to redress the balance. As a child I brought home every neglected animal I could find and I did three paper rounds to pay for the keep of my ever growing and varied menagerie. At my secondary school I refused to take part in biology classes, where we were required to dissect animals, and my poor mother had a visit from an irate headmistress complaining that my behaviour was hindering the progress of her classes.

My school-leaving coincided with the arrival on the Isle of Sheppey of an animal laboratory, and I took a job there. What I witnessed in the laboratory was the last straw and started me off on my adult life of rebellion on behalf of animals. Since that time I have never stopped at anything short of violence in my efforts to expose the mistreatment of animals. Violence I would never condone. Militancy in itself can achieve significant results, but violence never does and usually reacts against its cause.

One of the most successful campaigns in which I have been involved was the closing down of the Club Row animal market in London. Opened over one hundred years ago, this market specialised in selling animals as pets and was a favourite place for the public to visit on Sunday mornings. The conditions were disgraceful; puppies and kittens a few weeks old, birds and other domestic and exotic species were offered for sale, and at the end of the day's trading the council trucks would come to clean up. Frequently they would find, and have to take away, cardboard boxes containing unsold kittens and puppies left behind by uninterested stallholders. It was just like a scene out of Dickens.

The first time I went there I determined that the market should be closed down and I contacted the RSPCA, who told me they had the place under surveillance. This, I felt, was not good enough, and together with some friends I planned a campaign with the object of getting the market closed. To be realistic, we estimated this would take three to four years of constant effort, and my first step was to tell the local police of our intentions and assure them our demonstrations would be peaceful. We then approached the local council with a formal request to close the market. That, of course, was refused.

For three and a half years we then went to Club Row every Sunday morning. The public support was encouraging, but we soon realised that we needed publicity in the media, for which gimmicks were essential. So we bought tough tungsten chains and padlocks and chained ourselves across the road, from lamppost to lamppost, which prevented the dealers from setting up their stalls. We were often arrested for obstruction, the press gave us excellent coverage each time, and after pleading guilty we were fined and released. After a long campaign, we got the local council to debate our complaint against the market, but with no satisfaction. (The chairman had a brother who was a stallholder.) Clearly, more drastic measures were necessary, so we attended the next meeting of the council when our complaint was on the agenda again, and when the meeting was concluded – again with no satisfaction – we chained and padlocked ourselves right across the chamber, so that none of the councillors could leave.

Over the three and a half years, the police were very understanding, considering the trouble we caused. In the first winter, which was extremely cold, we had the frustration of being restricted to one side of the road and were unable to reach the young animals on the other side, who were visibly shivering with cold. The only answer was to stop the dealers arriving, and this led to what became known as our Tate and Lyle run. We found out where the dealers lived and went round the night before, putting sugar in the tanks of their trucks. We thought we had kept this ploy a secret, but one morning, when no trucks arrived on time, the chief inspector came up to me and asked, 'Have you been at your Tate and Lyle runs again?'

As the pace quickened, things began to get very nasty. Dealers started to repay our visits. They came to our homes, and when they came to mine, they killed all the birds in my aviary. However, we were not to be stopped and always had plenty of new ideas. On one occasion we started a noisy row among ourselves to distract attention. Police rushed over to discipline us, and while the stallholders backed them up with applause and advice, we sent a small group over the road to rescue shivering puppies.

During the campaign I was arrested eighteen times for crossing the road, and the police ran out of courts. It is a rule that a person can only be tried once before the same magistrate, to allay any suggestion of prejudice, so after running out of magistrates at Thames Magistrates' Court, they moved us to Wells Street, where we soon exhausted the supply, too. We also introduced a system for use at weekend arrests, when young probationer police officers were on duty. We would give our names as animals, our addresses as those of factory farms or laboratories, and occupations to match. Thus, a court would be surprised to hear an accused announced as 'Brown Rat. Unilever Research Unit. Occupation: LD50 test.'

In a way, I felt sorry for the police, who had files of complaints against them, for every time we were arrested we put in a complaint against the senior officer present. This was always the chief inspector, whose case had to be investigated by a superintendent, and it soon became clear that they could not cope with the weight of complaints. So finally I was invited up to Bethnal Green police station and asked to be reasonable and call off the complaints. I agreed, if in return they would ask the Home Office to close the market on the grounds that it could not be satisfactorily policed. More press features and an organised march of 5,500 people from Club Row to Downing Street, where we handed in a petition, finally achieved the objective.

When the market finally closed down, we had a celebration. The police joined in and we all wore funny hats, but I shall always believe that the police were rejoicing mainly because we were going away. I must say, however, that a curious relationship had grown up between us. For instance, there was a pub nearby which was used for illegal trading in birds, and periodically it would be raided. When a raid was planned, the police would ask if we would kindly move our demonstration a hundred yards down the road to assist them! The closure of Club Row, triumph though it was for the rights of the animals, was only the first step in the campaign which eventually led to this type of market being closed all over the country.

In the last two years the Christian Consultative Council for Animal Welfare, of which I am a member, has mounted a regular prayer vigil outside a primate laboratory in south London, as part of our Primate Action campaign. This, too, in a different way, has given the police authorities food for thought. No kind of protest demonstration could be less violent or aggressive than a prayer meeting, and when local complaints began to reach the police, they thundered down, in their usual fashion, to find a quiet group of twenty or so people standing with heads bowed in prayer. An officer approached one of our leading members, a man of the cloth, and quietly whispered, 'Excuse me, sir, you are not supposed to be here.' 'That's all right, officer,' came the reply, 'I am only here in spirit.' For nearly two years, on the second Sunday every month, we held our vigil – the police in attendance but anxious not to interrupt prayers – and I am happy to say that the publicity attending our efforts produced results. Although the primates are still there, conditions have been greatly improved and the campaign has not been wasted.

There are so many aspects of human mistreatment of animals, and what any individual can achieve is but a drop in the ocean. Nevertheless, conscience demands that we cannot stand by and be passive. When I toured round a number of catteries a while back, I was appalled at the conditions in many of them – and at the apparent lack of interest shown by the owners of the cats who used them. For this reason I opened my own cat hotel in Minster, where I live, and this makes an opportunity to show what can be done to provide happy and comfortable conditions for cats in boarding.

53
MIRABELLE
by Sheila Walker CBE JP

Sheila Walker is Vice-Chairman of the Council for the Preservation of Rural England and Membership Secretary for CPRE in Northamptonshire. From 1975 to 1980 she was Chief Commissioner of the Girl Guides Association and for eleven years she was a Justice of the Peace in Nottingham.

Mrs Walker has four children and twelve grandchildren, and a twenty-eight-year-old gander called the Brigadier, who is her constant companion.

The little black cat sat on the bank that sloped down to the canal. She was very thin and bedraggled. As I walked down the towpath towards her with the dogs, she slipped across the path in front of us and into the dense undergrowth the other side. Another time, seeing us approach, she ran up a tree overhanging the canal and watched us with her scared green eyes. It was the first time I had seen her clearly and I spoke to her softly, but she only climbed higher and when we came back a little later she had disappeared again. We saw her several times and I was saddened by her fear.

A terrible winter followed – thick snow, bitter winds, driving sleet and ice on the canal so thick we could walk down the middle of it and see a new world in the banks which could never be seen from the towpath. We stocked the big bird table two or three times every day; birds waited in all the nearby bushes and trees to descend on it before I was more than a few feet away. One morning a cock pheasant was sitting on it, eating corn and bread and fat, and one evening the little black cat was there, drinking the water and eating whatever she could before she saw me watching, jumped off and crept away into a hedge.

The kitchen door, with a big glass pane, opened into a large, open-fronted porch, where Miss Pigge the guinea pig's hutch was protected from the weather. When the cement floor was being put down, the dogs' front paws had been carefully pressed into it, and as far as I know the impressions are still there today. Out in this porch I put a bowl of milk and another of fresh mince, knowing some bird or animal would welcome it and hoping it would be found by the little black cat. I also put a box with straw and an old jersey in it under the table there – at least it was dry and out of the wind. Every morning the bowls were empty, and one morning when I opened the back door a black shadow streaked from the box under the table, out into the snow and away.

And so it went on, week after week. Every evening I would put the food and milk out and stand watching through the glass of the kitchen door till she came and wolfed it down, and every morning the box had been slept in again. Winter died away and spring came, and the little black cat's coat lost some of its spikiness as she filled out with at least one good meal a day. One evening, I put down her food and stood in the open door a few feet away while she ate, and later I stayed nearer to the bowls and talked to her. If I moved, she was gone, but over the weeks she grew more confident and would even have a wash before she left the porch. Then she took to waiting for me to take it out to her, forcing herself to resist the urge to run when I opened the door.

It was early summer before I put the back of my hand down, so slowly, talking all the time with nonsense endearments about 'brave little black plum pussies', and it happened. She rubbed her face against my hand, let it gently stroke her head and down her spine and burst into a frenzy of purring, butting against my hand, twining round my legs, purring for more till I wondered if she had ever purred before. After that it was easy; she came when I called and finally followed me into the house. She was not afraid when the dogs gushed and giggled over her at first, and they all accepted one another happily.

But the little black plum remained terrified of any loud noise. The washing machine, Hoover, mower or a car outside sent her streaking to the top of the nearest tree or away down the fields. What was her story, we wondered.

Months later, a group of schoolchildren came to the door. Plum was sitting in the hall when I opened it, but as soon as she saw them she arched her back, spitting and cursing at them before dashing away. 'It's our cat!' cried one small girl. 'Don't let her near you. She's fierce! She'll bite and scratch you. We had to turn her out ages ago and our dad tried to kill her.' So I called on the child's mother and heard how it all began.

Her husband worked at a Canadian Air Force base some miles away. One day, after a massive transport plane from Canada had been unloaded, they found a shoe-box, tied with string, lying on its side at the back of the hold. Someone threw it out of the plane to the ground below and some hours later it was opened. Inside was one terrified, starving black kitten who managed to run for cover. They tried, albeit half-heartedly, to catch her. They put food down if they saw her and forgot her if they didn't, and she lived rough on the base for some months till the man found her asleep in an old box in one of the hangers. He covered it with his coat, put it in his car and drove her home as a pet for his six children. The poor little cat, all her fears reawakened by being confined in a box again and the terrifying sound of an engine, was greeted with shouts of excitement as eager youngsters tried to pick her up, and she fought for her life with tooth and claw before escaping to the woods. 'We don't want her back,' I was told. 'She's dangerous. My husband went out after her with a gun but he never found her.' I was delighted.

Someone suggested that she was a French Canadian cat and understood French better than English, but she had been too small to understand anything when a human had crushed her into that little box, tied it with string against her struggles and tossed it, probably laughing, on top of the freight in the plane. She was only two or three months old and perhaps alone for the first time in her life when it roared and creaked on its icy nightmare journey from Canada to the English Midlands, and then the box had been thrown to the ground. How did she survive?

Now she was beginning to feel safe and to forget, but in deference to her origins we christened her Mirabelle, a small, black French plum, and we loved her dearly for the fifteen years of devotion and happiness that she gave us.

54
THE STREETWISE DOG
by Mark Wallington

When Mark Wallington undertook a five hundred mile trek around the western coastline from Minehead to Poole, he borrowed a dog as companion. The following extracts from his book 500 Mile Walkies *present an amusing but sympathetic picture of their relationship and of the lovable and distinctive character of the dog of the London streets.*

Boogie isn't my dog. When I said I borrowed everything for the journey I meant everything.

Boogie lives with Sean who used to live with my sister. They had a squat in South London. Walking home from the fish and chip shop one evening, Sean noticed two shiny black eyes peering from beneath a kerbed taxi cab. There, huddled against a wheel, lay the abandoned baby Boogie.

Even then he was a strange-looking creature. According to a local shopkeeper he was an only child, and yet he'd still been discarded as the runt of the litter. Sean picked him up and immediately Boogie zapped him with one of those lambent looks that would in later life earn him extra helpings of breakfast. Sean was helpless. He cradled the pitiful mite in his dufflecoat pocket next to a warm piece of rock and carried him home.

A dog's upbringing on the council estates of Stockwell and Brixton is a tough one. Boogie would get beaten up daily, usually by cats, but like everything that survives down there he soon grew streetwise and by his first birthday he was a jet black spiv strutting about the streets of London like a barrow boy.

As Sean's lifestyle improved so did Boogie's; come to think of it, so did my sister's. They crossed the river and moved to West Hampstead. They paid rent and even acquired a spare room – a dangerous move when there are people like me about. I came to stay a weekend and left a year later. It was during this time I came to understand, as well as is possible, what a freak of nature Boogie is.

To call him a mongrel is an insult to mongrels. When I first met him I wasn't even sure he was a dog. He had a thinly wrapped frame, two-feet high and arched like a hyena. Perched on top is the face of an imp and a pair of highly original ears. He looks like a cross between a fox and a Morris 1000.

In defence of his looks, Sean claims Boogie is a dog with character, which is true, a horrible one. His calamitous infancy has left him devious and insecure, a fickle animal who'll go home with anyone carrying a takeaway curry. He spends his time hanging around the bookies and watching television in shop windows. He can operate pelican crossings. He jumps on buses and goes up the West End. He has a taxi driver's Knowledge and can understand rhyming slang. He thinks the Kennel Club is a night spot. He prefers pavements to grass. He cocks his leg on lampposts rather than trees. His only experience of the countryside is the time he got run over by a Luton-bound Green-line bus. In short, Boogie and nature have nothing in common.

Yet when I needed a dog to take on this walk, he was the only candidate. The idea of letting this product of concrete and carbon monoxide loose on the natural high drama of the southwest coast was irresistible. It was introducing the beast to beauty and it immediately gave the journey a whole new dimension.

* * *

Combe Martin's claim to fame is as the second longest village in Britain, which as claims to fame go has to be one of the most stupid and does nothing but make you wonder what the longest is.

If it is Britain's second longest village then it's probably because the combe it sits in is Britain's second narrowest. The one and only street winds inland for about two miles. We walked a hundred yards of it until I found a grocery store where I bought our supplies for the day. These I promptly dropped all over the pavement, sending rivulets of milk rushing to the nearest drain. Back I went for a replacement pint, while Boogie, inspired by this accident, decided to give the second longest village in Britain a special performance of his very own milk bottle trick.

This, predictably, involves drinking the milk rather than spilling it and requires a sleight of paw taught him by Black Jack Jake the one-eyed whippet of SW9. Black Jack ran a protection racket on the Stockwell Park Estate and struck terror in every resident, man and beast. He was wanted for three separate pavement violations and rumour had it that he once caught rabies but had 'shrugged it off'. He lost his eye the night he and three of the Lambeth Labradors went to break his brother out of Battersea.

Anyway, the milk bottle trick: the paws cradle the bottle and the tongue pierces the foil top and slurps out the cream. The paws then deftly tilt the bottle and the tongue does some more slurping. Just before the bottle overbalances, the paws let go and the bottle totters back to its original position, half a pint diminished. The dog then scarpers as the lady of the house, short of something to put on her cereal, emerges in her dressing gown and discovers the crime. The first thing she'll do is look up and chances are she'll see a sparrow: 'Bleedin' birds!' she'll mutter and then shake her fist and shuffle back inside. Incredible, half a pint missing and still the birds get the blame. Birds with straws perhaps.

Away from his home patch Boogie wasn't so discreet. As I came out of the store for the second time, I saw a group of Combe Martin's finest housewives watching in silence as Boogie worked his way from bottle to bottle, doorstep to doorstep, up the street. It wasn't anger the ladies displayed so much as disbelief. I apologised profusely, placed my new pint down on the first step, ran back into the shop and bought the appropriate number of replacements from a shopkeeper who was by now convinced I was up to something but couldn't work out what, other than that it involved milk. Then I grabbed the white moustachio'd Boogie and together we bowed out of the second longest village in Britain and adjourned to the beach, where we ate large quantities of bread and Winalot.

* * *

On the morning of 28 May, the campers and caravanners of Seaton were treated to a rare sight: Boogie immersed in water.

Having been on the move now for three weeks, his grooming was unlikely to win him any lucrative advertising contracts. His underbelly played host to a jungle of parasites, mostly tics, which reappeared as fast as I could pull them off. His feet were the texture of Brillo pads and his coat a compost heap of birds' nests, brambles, soup, Kennomeat, mud and dung from any of the following: sheep, pig, cow, horse, hedgehog. You name it and he'd rolled in it. Never one to leave anywhere without a souvenir, as we left our campsite in the woods he opted for an early morning roll in a good-sized cowpat of nauseous viscosity. It was more than I could bear. It was time he had a bath.

Easier said than done.

Boogie's hatred of water is legendary. The only method devised to get him into a tub is too complicated to explain here but suffice to say it involves a straitjacket and both sets of neighbours.

I sat on Seaton's grey beach and stripped off to my shorts. Boogie sat on the sand, nose raised, tuned in to some bacon frying in a distant caravan. Whistling nonchalantly, I strolled over to him and in a flash I'd grabbed a leg and was dragging him seawards. If I wanted him to go somewhere that badly, Boogie deduced, then chances were he didn't want to go there, and he dug his three remaining heels into the sand like anchors. Risking a mawling, I picked him up and struggled into the sea up to my knees. I dropped him and he was back on dry land without disturbing the water. I ran out and chased him over the beach. Lunging, I caught the end of a slippery tail and pulled myself up, then, gripping him in a bear hug I returned to the water. This time I didn't risk releasing him, I just rolled over and held him under. We rolled over again and he held me under. By now campers were appearing at the top of the beach clutching fried egg sandwiches and watching the contest. A woman trotted along the shoreline on horseback. 'Morning!' she called and beamed.

'Morning!' I replied, going under for the third time.

When the battle was over, I lay on the beach, panting. Boogie studied his body, now ninety per cent dog and only ten per cent muck, having been inversely proportioned ten minutes previously. At the water's edge a little boy stood wearing a rubber ring and contemplating the turbid slick that now floated to the surface.

55
MONGREL DOGS
An interview with Oliver Warman RBA

Educated at Stowe, Exeter University and Balliol College, Oxford, Oliver Warman spent the first twenty years of his working life as a Welsh Guardsman, taking up painting seriously on his return to civilian life. His work has been exhibited at the Royal Academy and many other prestigious societies, and he has had one-man exhibitions in London, the provinces, Stockholm, Helsinki and Gothenburg. He is now Chief Executive of the Federation of British Artists.

Oliver Warman has a healthy respect and affection for the mongrel dog and tells of some of his unusual experiences with his four-legged companions.

I have always loved small dogs and I started off, at the age of eleven, with a dog which is best described as a sort of Jack Russell, there being a suspicion of Heinz 57 varieties in his pedigree. In those days young men used to wear jackets and I had a tweed jacket – probably a hand-me-down – with big pockets, and this pseudo-Jack Russell loved to sit inside. It made him feel important, to be taller than other dogs.

One day I took him to church in my jacket, and being bored by the sermon, I let him free. He found his way into one of those large Victorian heating pipes, crawled quite a long way down it and poked his head out through an aperture. He looked straight at an elderly lady, who was startled out of her wits. No doubt she was hoping to make contact with her Maker and instead my dog appeared. I got into quite a lot of trouble over that episode. The church warden was sent for. He had to turn off the heating valves to get the dog out and quite a party developed. After that day, my mother always inspected me before leaving for church.

A dog is a boy's best friend and when you come home for the school holidays, you find he is the only one you really like or who shows real interest in you. When I became a soldier I had what looked like an Aberdeen terrier; her mother had had a misalliance with someone unknown. My job in those days was to train National Service recruits. I was in charge of potential officers and a photograph was taken of me and my dog, whom I called Sally. It always struck me as amusing that the photographer captioned the picture 'Captain Warman and Sally the dog'. The last two words were a shade superfluous!

Those potential officers had to try harder than anyone else and we gave them a very rough time. Sally played her part with an excess of enthusiasm and used to chase them over the ranges, biting their calves and making life generally difficult for them. But it was not only the recruits who were her victims. One day I was sitting in my office when I caught a glimpse of a pair of stockinged feet passing my open door. Suspicious at all times of young potential officers being up to no good, I crept to the door and put my head round. To my surprise, it was my company sergeant-major – a six-foot Welsh Guardsman, with two rows of campaign medals – and he was about to leap on Sally the dog, who was sitting on the steps contemplating an immaculate boot in front of her. I heard him shout: 'Come here, you black-faced, four-legged. . . ., I'll wring your neck!' Sally the dog had stolen his best boots.

After Sally the dog came Zeta, another 'sort of Jack Russell' but with very short legs. Zeta came to a very sticky end because she could not really work out in her head that she was always supposed to be with me. Instead, canine logic told her that the place to be was close to the cookhouse dustbins, where a variety of bones and the delicious remains of the officers' mess dinners were to be found. The inevitable happened when the driver of the provisions truck reversed and the dog was in the way. It was very sad; Zeta was a sweet little creature.

After that experience I decided my next dog must be a little bigger. At the local animal sanctuary in Newbury I found a Welsh mountain sheepdog. She had been maltreated and was very happy to find a new home. We used to go for long walks together and this dog had a very keen nose. Bess, as she was named, would dash into the nearest coppice and flush out the birds, and this led me into constant trouble with the local farmers. They were all immensely rich and used to indulge in enormous shoots, and they naturally objected to Bess's uncontrolled activities. I had regular complaints, asking me to keep my dog off their land and restrain her from disturbing the wildlife, but nothing would persuade her to mend her ways. Bess was about ten years old when I took her on. I had her for five years and she died of old age at fifteen.

My next dog was a sex maniac, a Border terrier whom I christened Hercules. By this time I had moved to London, and when he was quite young I remember an embarrassing incident in Hyde Park. We were out for our daily walk around the Serpentine when he suddenly disappeared – a habit he had. I began, as usual, to call out 'Hercules! Hercules!' and, as usual, everybody within earshot stopped and turned round, no doubt expecting at least to see a Great Dane or an Irish wolfhound. Instead, they witnessed the sight of a small dog having an impassioned liaison with a Cairn terrier.

By chance, I happened to know the owner of the Cairn, and duly learned that the affaire had produced a Cairn/Border terrier puppy called Sebastian. So, when Hercules departed to the great kennel in the sky, I adopted Sebastian. After all, like Lloyd George, I knew his father!

Alas, Sebastian inherited his father's weakness, but as he grew to maturity he calmed down, discovering that there are things in life more rewarding than chasing female dogs. I lived in Cornwall for a time, when I had a boat, and Sebastian became convinced that he was a naval officer. My boat was shaped like a German lady, broader than she was high, and Sebastian would strut around the deck, looking terribly important. When we were on the move, he would sit bolt upright in the bows, looking neither to left nor right but straight ahead. Sebastian, I am grateful to say, is still with us.

He is now thirteen, and I think that when he is called to his Maker, I shall go back to having a sort of Jack Russell. Their morals, for some undefined reason, are not so bad as some others.

Mongrels seem so much more intelligent – and certainly more healthy – than pedigree dogs. I did once have a Sealyham, but she had eczema very badly and I decided then that pedigree dogs were not for me. The mongrel is more hardy, and needs to be, as he has to make his own way in life.

56
SALUKI – THE
ARABIAN GAZELLE-HOUND
An interview with Hope Waters

*Hope Waters is the leading British breeder of Salukis and an
international authority on the breed. She is married to Lieutenant
Commander David Waters* RN, *a distinguished historian, and in
1969 they published the definitive book on the history of Salukis
–* The Saluki in History, Art and Sport *– with a second edition
in 1984.*

*Mrs Waters tells how she became a breeder by sheer chance and
recalls some of her unusual experiences.*

As a child I lived right in the middle of Dartmoor. My only
companions were my father's animals, and I depended on
them entirely for my pleasures and for company. It was a
lonely life, riding to school three and half miles away on a
pony, and I broke away as soon as I reasonably could. My
mother had died when I was very young, my father was
entirely wrapped up in running his estate and breeding Irish
terriers, and I was glad to get away to live with friends and
earn my living until I married.

My first husband, Rick, was the brother of my present
husband, David, and like him, was a naval officer. Soon after
we married he was appointed to a ship in Malta, where I
accompanied him. One day, when he was away on Fleet exercises, I came across a starving dog in the street. I followed
her to the vicinity of a fisherman's hut on the waterfront,
where she hopefully went for scraps. The following day, on
my husband's return, we visited the fisherman, who said we
could take her away as she was homeless. She was so hungry

that as we walked her home, she seized and, before we could stop her, gulped down most of a dead pigeon she found in the gutter.

We shared a house with another naval officer and his wife and they objected strongly to our bringing in this appalling, filthy dog, especially when I insisted on bathing her in the shared bathroom! Actually, the wretched dog was in such a hopeless condition that we decided she would have to be put down, but Miss Knight, an English lady who had a humane killer and attended to the problem of stray dogs, was on holiday. By the time she returned, a month later, our Melita, as we called her, was a healthy, respectable dog and we had grown so fond of her that she was not to be put down. She was a big dog, half Maltese pointer and half Maltese rabbit dog (Pharaoh Hound), and careful feeding, grooming and attention had transformed her. She accompanied us when I followed the Fleet to Alexandria, and then back to England, and I kept her for twelve years until she died soon after the end of the war.

Tragedy struck during the war when my husband Rick was drowned and I was alone in England with two young children and Melita. In 1945 David, my brother-in-law, returned to England and, having no relatives and nowhere to go, he came to stay with me. We married in 1946 and have enjoyed a truly happy and fulfilled life ever since.

We moved to Bury in West Sussex and decided to have a sporting breed. No doubt breeding was in my blood through my father, and I was anxious to have a top-class hound with a view to showing as a hobby. My husband and I had read about Salukis and studied their history. They originated in the region of Arabia around 5000 BC. What could well be one appears in a fresco of that period showing a hunter with a long-nosed, long-tailed hound and, by 3000 BC, in the heyday of Ur, they are clearly identifiable as some were embalmed with their masters. The Saluki is the only dog an Arab will touch; it is said that if the shadow of another dog falls across his food, he will throw it away. In the desert, Bedouin women will suckle a Saluki puppy, if necessary. It is also the only dog that has no smell. The Saluki is the fundamental gaze-hound, hunting by sight rather than by scent. They will see for long distances and it is said that in the desert light they can see for as far as seven miles. For the past thousand years they have been trained to hunt with hawks. The hawk will spot the game and hover above it. The hound will chase and arrest it, pinning it down until the Arab rides up and despatches it.

About AD 1900 Salukis began to be popular in England, when Lord Amherst's daughter had them brought here and, in the 1914–18 war, army officers in Mesopotamia joined Arabs in hunting with them. After the war some were privileged to bring home Salukis presented to them. Finally, in 1923, the Saluki Club was formed and the breed was recognised by the Kennel Club.

Having decided on Salukis, I bought a black and tan bitch puppy and, soon after, her sister needed a home. Then fate took a hand. A friend of mine, Elizabeth Wyndham, who had been working in the diplomatic service in Berlin, returned home with a Saluki bitch and her litter. In quarantine all died from hardpad, except the mother and two of the puppies, one of which was a dog called Uki. Elizabeth moved near to us, and Uki took a fancy to us, paying us unauthorised and unannounced visits several times a day by jumping our double gates.

This I did not favour, as I might have a bitch in season in the garden, and I vigorously complained. Finally, when Elizabeth decided to move to London, Uki was to be put down, so inevitably I offered to give him a home. I did not want a dog – the complication with bitches around was too great – but I took him, and that is the reason why I became famous as a Saluki breeder. Uki was a magnificent stud dog. I had a white bitch whom I bred to him, and from this mating came the only Saluki to be awarded Best Bitch and Reserve Best in Show at Crufts. This was out of over eight thousand dogs in 1964.

My life seems to have been bound up with these hounds, and the radical plans my husband and I have made for the future originate from a Saluki encounter some thirty years ago. I went to a dog show at Brent, in north London, on my own with three Salukis. There, by overhearing a chance remark, I made friends with a young Canadian girl who was over here to help support her husband while he was at university. Carole gave me a hand with the dogs and revealed herself as very knowledgable and fond of the breed. I invited them to visit us in Sussex, we became firm friends and have since exchanged many visits between Sussex and Canada, where she now lives in British Columbia in beautiful country, alongside an eighty-mile lake. The upshot of the story is that we have bought a property next to hers and plan soon to spend the rest of our lives in Canada, taking our Salukis with us.

But the story does not end there. Last year I attended a show where the organisers had laid on a party to celebrate my forty years in the breed. The news reached a Canadian Saluki friend of ours and Carole's who was over here to attend a show. We met, and in the course of conversation we discovered that she had bought a property adjoining our new Canadian home, to which she was to move on her return, and so we will have another Saluki neighbour.

Finally, visiting us in Sussex, she admired a puppy of mine and took it back to Canada with her. She journeyed three thousand miles across the prairies and the Rockies with two horses and the Saluki pup, to our new community. It is indeed fortunate for me and for my marriage that David, my husband, is equally hooked!

57
REFLECTIONS
An interview with J. N. P. Watson

Educated at Eton and Sandhurst, Major Johnnie Watson served for twenty years in the Royal Horse Guards (Blues), until he was invalided out, and saw service in Cyprus, Egypt, Germany and Gibraltar. He commanded the Guards Independent Parachute Company and subsequently the Sovereign's Escort of Household Cavalry. Since then, as a writer and journalist, he has published books and articles on many aspects of wildlife and animal behaviour. A lifelong animal lover, he is host to five dogs at his Sussex home and he also maintains a very flourishing dovecot, a collection of ornamental wild fowl in a skilfully protected lake and a large goldfish pond.

Major Watson holds strong views on man's sad abuse of his responsibilities to the animal world.

One of my earliest childhood memories was of our cook spilling some burning fat out of a frying pan on to the head of a Siamese cat. In a short time its ear was completely frizzled down to nothing, and for the rest of its life it wept from one eye. I remember hours spent leaning my head against it in an attempt to comfort the poor thing.

It is fascinating to consider how events in childhood stay in the mind and can remain equally vivid even after more than fifty years. In 1936 the Crystal Palace burnt down, providing London with its biggest conflagration since the 1914 war and lighting up the whole of the capital and a large part of Kent and Surrey. I was a small boy at my prep school in Surrey and currently in the sick room, deep in the dog story *Jock of the Bushveldt* by Percy Fitzpatrick, when the sky lit up, giving me light to continue reading this dramatic yarn. It concluded with the story of his death and the final chapter opened with the words 'And Jock? I never saw my dog again.' As my emotions overcame me and the tears ran down my cheeks, the matron burst into the room, calling 'Quick, boys, look! The Crystal Palace is burning down.' To me, even today, the death of Jock is more vivid than the real demise of the Crystal Palace.

My family had a house in Chelsea and a country house in Sussex, and my very first memories of animals were of our bull terriers and Siamese cats being moved down from London to Sussex and back again with the family. I was, even then, an avid reader of Kipling and I used to pretend I was Mowgli from *Jungle Book*. My world was peopled with real and legendary animals and I would get terribly upset if I heard of any animal suffering. When the RSPCA opened a junior membership about that time, I was one of the first to join and I have been involved with animal welfare ever since.

In 1968, after twenty years as a professional soldier, I joined the staff of *Country Life* and one of my responsibilities was to write about nature reserves. This gave me the knowledge and experience to qualify for a Churchill Fellowship, which I was awarded in the context of animal welfare and wildlife conservation. I spent six weeks in the USA and Canada, hosted by local branches of the International Fund for Animal Welfare, and I saw some gruesome sights. I was particularly distressed to see, at first hand, evidence of the extreme cruelty involved in trapping for the wealthy fur trade.

It is a massive industry, involving first the trappers – men whose families for generations have depended on the trade for their livelihood. They are not, by any means, rich – the profits come at the other end of the process – and it was all started by the British, a fact which is not generally recognised. The original charter, giving licence to the Hudson Bay Company, was signed three hundred years ago by King Charles the Second.

Over twenty species of furred animals are trapped, killed and skinned for their pelts, from bears and sable down to the thousands of little muskrats which provide the pelts for the internationally popular musquash coats. They live on the edges of the marshes and are trapped by the hundreds in leg-hold devices. The International Fund for Animal Welfare has supported the introduction of a trap which drowns the animal when it is caught and thereby lessens the misery and pain. Officials of IFAW point out that there is no way in which the traffic can be stopped under present laws, especially when whole regions depend on it for employment. The only hope is to control it through newly imposed conditions, such as redesigned trapping methods. The macabre evidence of the trappers' trade is to be seen outside Toronto in the enormous warehouses, the size of aircraft hangers, where thousands of beautifully cured pelts hang, elegant and glamorous, awaiting export to those who will transform them into wearing apparel for people who are oblivious of the torture that is involved.

The Bible tells us that God gave man dominion over the earth and all living things on it, but the early theologians and church leaders who wrote the books of the Bible made little reference to man's responsibility to the lesser creatures. I believe that, at the Day of Judgement, if such a day ever comes, the first indictment will not so much concern man's inhumanity to man (which goodness knows is dreadful enough) as the proud pedestal, the position of omnipotence, upon which he has placed himself, at the tragic expense of all life on earth, including his own and that of his descendants.

Let me end on a lighter – and, I fear, a somewhat blasphemous – note. And let me add that the following account is entirely unembellished. A few years ago, when I embarked on my Churchill Fellowship in the United States and Canada, I read somewhere that the Pilgrim Fathers pledged themselves to be kind to all animals. But, having lost the reference, I enquired of the local representative of the International Fund for Animal Welfare in Boston whether he could put his finger on it. He said he, too, had read it, but could not remember where. 'Why don't you contact the Quaker office in Philadelphia?' he suggested. 'Or easier still, why not attend the Quaker service here in Boston tomorrow and ask the guy in charge there?'

I duly sat for an hour in the silent Quaker circle, and then put my question to the keeper of the old church. 'I don't know the answer,' he replied (over the customary Quaker coffee and biscuits) 'but . . .' – pointing to a woman in the corner – 'that lady transferred from the Episcopalians to the Quakers on account of animals. Try her.' So I did.

'I left the Episcopalians to come here because the Quakers have this deep reverence for all life and I guess I just got sick of some of the doings of *that man*,' the woman declared.

'What man?' I asked.

She looked at me as though I was an idiot. 'Why, Jesus Christ, naturally. First he had the Gadarene pigs fall very painfully over that cliff; then he fed the five thousand on fish that had been just gasping for life in those nasty nets on the shore of Lake Galilee; and then there was the Passover. He didn't give a damn for the throats of little lambs gettin' slit. He didn't give a cent for animals.'

'Well, the trouble is man has been given dominion over every—' I ventured.

'Exactly so,' she interrupted. 'That's why I'm a Quaker. They have more consideration, I guess.'

58

CONTENTED CHICKENS
An interview with Audrey Wise MP

Audrey Wise first entered Parliament in 1974 as the Member for Coventry South West which she represented until 1979. A keen worker for women's rights, she is also a member of War on Want, Labour Action for Peace, CND, Nicaragua Solidarity, and the Soil Association. She is now the Labour Member of Parliament for Preston.

Mrs Wise has little time for sentimentality towards animals, but she strongly advocates respect for their place in society and has a realistic and mutually advantageous relationship with her own free-range hens.

I am not an animal lover in the accepted sense but I think they should be treated with understanding and respect. I believe many species are grossly underestimated and we do not appreciate their usefulness and capacities. In this context I would specially mention dogs and the essential work they perform as guide dogs and sheepdogs.

When I was a small girl in the war years, my grandmother kept hens in her backyard. I remember how they made a noise at the crack of dawn each day, asking to be let out. I also remember vividly the hot mash she made for their daily meal. When I grew up I sometimes thought how nice it would be to have our own free-range eggs. However, I was not so keen on the hot mash idea, nor did I fancy the crack of dawn requirement!

Then two things happened. We were living in Stafford with a largish garden, and I read in a gardening magazine about the advantages of keeping hens in your greenhouse in winter.

We have a large greenhouse in which we grow a good crop of tomatoes, but I was still wondering about the daily hot mash until my husband asked: 'Who gave them hot mash in the jungle?' The second happening was that friends living in the country gave us their five hens. The die was cast.

The hens were far from their first youth, as hens' lives are generally reckoned. They were in fact entering their third season – a time when most of their sisters have been killed.

The experiment was fascinating. It was a very cold midwinter when the hens arrived, but they settled beautifully into the greenhouse with some straw bedding, and whatever the weather they loved to venture out, even in the snow. From these five oldish hens, in their first year with us, we recorded over twelve hundred eggs.

I read books about chicken-keeping and bought layers' pellets and mixed corn as recommended, but soon discovered that the pellets contained artificial colouring to colour the yolks! Hardly the thing for an advocate of organic food, so we dropped the pellets. Cabbage leaves give deep golden yolks, slugs are lovely protein (but we now have a garden shortage of slugs), mixed corn is fine, and their only preventive medication is crushed garlic in their drinking water. Not only do we enjoy an abundant supply of free-range eggs from happy hens, but our summer crop of tomatoes is better than ever and our greenhouse entirely pest free.

In the summer months our hens roam the garden and live in a smaller plastic doorless greenhouse, which can be moved from time to time, and we have learned much from studying these interesting creatures.

Some people say hens are stupid, but I disagree. Unless forced by arrogant humans, they never eat the wrong things and make themselves ill, which is more than can be said about the intelligent human race. If hens rummage among green leaves, they know just which ones to eat and which to leave alone. They will eat green caterpillars but not orange and black striped ones. We think this might be a colour warning, orange and black being the colour of wasps. You may not call that intelligence, but it is certainly functional, and considering the size of a hen's brain, I think they do very nicely. If we made equal use of our brains we'd live in a much better world.

Hens are friendly and gregarious, and they have individual temperaments. Some are more cautious than others, some will be much noisier, some quite bold. One hen we had would be perching on your foot as soon as you put a fork into the ground. They are very particular about their sleeping arrangements. We originally provided perches for them, but we found they prefer to sleep on top of an old chest of drawers. Five will share one chest top, but if you have more than one chest they must be the same height because hens dislike seeing other hens above them.

Laying arrangements too are interesting. We made a nesting box out of a tea chest turned on its side, with a curtain made from strips of carpet along the open front. They straightaway adopted it, and they like to lay their eggs in the dark and in private. Occasionally two hens will occupy the box together, but mostly one at a time.

We decided not to have a cock, out of consideration for the neighbours, so we buy in young birds to replace those which die of old age. There is no evidence of a pecking order, but the babies know their place. They keep out of the way of the older hens, and even go to bed earlier. Then, gradually, as they grow older, they integrate into the social system.

Animals are not machines. It is immoral to treat them as though they are, but they are clearly regarded this way by battery egg and chicken producers. It is not done to produce cheap food, but simply to make money.

Nature will take revenge on people for the cruel misuse of power involved in keeping hens cramped and crippled in small cages. And from the consumer's point of view there is no comparison in the final product – the egg.

Our hens also help in the production of our vegetables by enriching the compost which we make and use. A great many people could keep hens in their suburban gardens without undue work, or nuisance to their neighbours, and enjoy the luxury of real home-produced free-range eggs while providing a happy environment for industrious and friendly hens – a model of partnership between people and animals.